GETTING GRAPHIC!

Comics for Kids

MICHELE GORMAN

With a foreword by Jeff Smith, creator of *Bone*,
and original comic art by Jimmy Gownley, creator of *Amelia Rules*

Linworth
Books

Professional Development Resources for K-12
Library Media and Technology Specialists

Library of Congress Cataloging-in-Publication Data

Gorman, Michele.
  Getting graphic! : comics for kids / Michele Gorman ; with a foreword by Jeff Smith, ; and original comic art by Jimmy Gownley.
      p. cm.
  Includes bibliographical references and index.
  ISBN-13: 978-1-58683-327-5 (pbk.)
  ISBN-10: 1-58683-327-8 (pbk.)
  1. Comic books, strips, etc.--History and criticism. 2. Comic books and children. I. Gownley, Jimmy. II. Title.
  PN6710.G678 2008
  741.509--dc22

                                    2007035033

Cynthia Anderson: Editor
Carol Simpson: Editorial Director
Judi Repman: Consulting Editor
Christine Weiser: Project Editor

Published by Linworth Publishing, Inc.
3650 Olentangy River Road, Suite 250
Columbus, Ohio 43214

TRADEMARK INFORMATION
Rather than put a trademark symbol with every occurrence of a trademarked name, we are using the names only in an editorial fashion and to the benefit of the trademark owner, with no intention of infringement of the trademark.

COVER ART
Cover of TINY TYRANT by Lewis Trondheim and Fabrice Parme. Copyright Lewis Trondheim. Used with permission from First Second Books.

Mouse Guard: Fall 1152 is copyright 2007 by David Petersen. All rights reserved.

ISBN: 1-58683-327-8

5 4 3 2 1

Table of Contents

Table of Illustrations i

Dedication ii

Acknowledgments ii

Foreword: Jeff Smith iii

"Amelia Rules! On the Bandwagon"
    by Jimmy Gownley iv

About the Author. viii

Introduction ix

Section 1: Comic Fiction for Younger Readers 1

Section 2: Manga for Younger Readers.............37

Section 3: Comic Nonfiction for Younger Readers....57

Appendix A: Glossary 77

Appendix B: Online Resource Guides 78

Appendix C: Professional Books about Graphic
    Novels and Comic Books.........................79

Index 80

Table of Illustrations

Section 1:

Amelia Rules! Volume 3: Superheroes
    by Jimmy Gownley.................................5

BABYMOUSE: ROCK STAR! by Jennifer L.
    Holm and Matthew Holm 7

Bone, Volume 1: Out From Boneville
    by Jeff Smith...9

The Courageous Princess
    by Rod Espinosa...................................12

King Arthur and the Knights of the
    Round Table adapted by M.C Hall,
    illustrated by C.E. Richards 16

Lions, Tigers, and Bears, Volume 1:
    Fear and Pride by Mike Bullock
    and Jack Lawrence 19

Oddly Normal, Volume 1
    by Otis Frampton.................................22

Owly, Volume 3: Flying Lessons
    by Andy Runton 24

Polly and the Pirates by Ted Naifeh 26

Polo: The Runaway Book
    by Régis Faller 2

Robot Dreams by Sara Varon.........................28

Twisted Journeys #2: Escape from Pyramid X
    by Dan Jolley and Matt Wendt..............34

The World of Quest by Jason T. Kruse.........36

Section 2:

How to Read Manga Diagram 40

Hikaru No Go, Volume 1 by Yumi Hotta ..44

Yotsuba&!, Volume 1
    by Kiyohiko Azuma 47

Mail Order Ninja, Volume 1 by Joshua Elder
    and Erich Owen....................................51

Warriors, Volume 1: The Lost Warrior by
Erin Hunter, Dan Jolley.......................54

Section 3:

Amaterasu: Return of the Sun:
    A Japanese Myth by Paul D. Storrie
    and Ron Randall 58

The Battle of Iwo Jima: Guerilla Warfare
    in the Pacific by Larry Hama and
    Anthony Williams 60

Clan Apis by Jay Hosler 63

To Dance: A Ballerina's Graphic Novel
    by Siena Cherson Siegel and
    Mark Siegel...65

The Shocking World of Electricity
    with Max Axiom, Super Scientist by Liam
    O'Donnell, Richard Dominguez, and
    Charles Barnett III 73

 # Dedication

This one is for my niece and nephew,
Grayson William and Grace Erin.
May you guys always have books in your lives.

 # Acknowledgments

Like a child, it takes a village to raise a book. This one would not exist if it weren't for the support of the following people:

Marlene Woo-Lun, for the white water river rafting trip (again, like a child, this book had to be conceived somewhere!).

Everyone at Linworth Publishing, including Christine Weiser and Donna King, for helping me make this book a reality in such a short period of time.

Jimmy Gownley, for his amazing cover art and original comic. Your work inspired me to write this book!

Jeff Smith, for his foreword. Thank you for coming back for the second round. As always, your work sets the bar for graphic novels for readers of all ages.

Bill Corder, for his contributions and feedback.

Everyone in the general and comics publishing industry (including those of you who work in editing, administration, marketing, and sales) for always keeping me up-to-date about what's new and hot in your world.

My librarian friends in the comic world, especially Robin Brenner, Mike Pawuk, and Kat Kan for all the support and feedback.

My friends in the comics publishing industry, especially Ron Espinoza, Rich Johnson, Joe Keatinge, Thea Kuticka, Michael Martens, Terry and Robyn Moore, Janna Morishima, Chris Oarr, Alan Payne, Hillery Pastovich, Kasia Piekarz, John Shableski, Mark Siegel, and Chris Staros.

My inner circle: Janet, Marin, Paula, Sarah, and Tricia. None of this would be much fun without you guys.

Everyone at ImaginOn, especially the Loft Staff, for putting up with me.

My family and friends, for also putting up with me and loving me in spite of the fact that I work all the time.

My colleagues at the Public Library of Charlotte & Mecklenburg County.

And finally to the young people I have the good fortune to work with every day. Thank you for reminding me why I do what I do.

Comics are changing. Not only have they moved from the newsstands and drugstores of the 1940s to 21st-century bookstores, schools, and libraries, but they have changed on the inside as well. Early comics were commercial products cranked out in an assembly line fashion on tight schedules, but the modern field of comics attracts many thoughtful artists wishing to create lasting works.

Once thought to be the province of children, the medium has grown to include complex and sophisticated stories—some more suitable for young eyes than others— just as in any other art form or popular entertainment.

That's why Michele Gorman has created *Getting Graphic! Comics for Kids.* There are a lot of talented creators making books for every possible age group. Use this guide to help you select the appropriate books for your library and classroom.

There's something about the combination of words and pictures that appeals especially to children. They read comics because they want to, and you can't do any better than that.

Jeff Smith
Creator of the *Bone* graphic novel series

"Amelia Rules! On the Bandwagon" by Jimmy Gownley

UNFORTUNATELY, REGGIE IS IN FOR ANOTHER SHOCK, WHEN HE ARRIVES AT HIS SCHOOL LIBRARY...

About the Author

Michele Gorman is the Teen Services Manager of ImaginOn, a collaborative venture of the Public Library of Charlotte & Mecklenburg County and the Children's Theater of Charlotte in Charlotte, North Carolina. At ImaginOn, cutting-edge library services, innovative educational programs, and new generation technology meet award-winning professional theater to bring stories to life through extraordinary experiences that challenge, inspire, and excite young minds. In addition to working full-time as a teen librarian, Michele is also a freelance writer and renowned national speaker. Her books include *Getting Graphic! Using Graphic Novels to Promote Literacy with Preteens and Teens* (Linworth Publishing 2003) and the third edition of *Connecting Young Adults and Libraries* (Neal-Schuman Publishing 2004), co-written with Patrick Jones and Tricia Suellentrop. Michele is a "Teenage Riot" columnist for *School Library Journal* and the "Getting Graphic" columnist for *Library Media Connection*. You can find out more about her on her Web site: <www.comixlibrarian.com>.

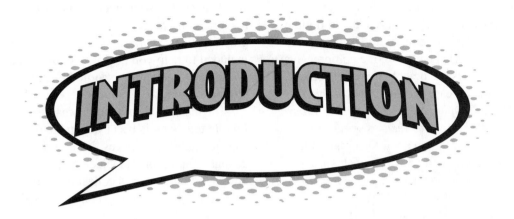

When my first book, *Getting Graphic! Using Graphic Novels to Promote Literacy with Preteens and Teens*, came out in 2003, the graphic novel format was still being judged for its worthiness in public and school libraries. Over the years, many things have changed with regard to both the public and professional perception of graphic novels and comic books. For me, the most important change has been at the hands of librarians, who have willingly accepted and embraced books created in a comic format. Once shunned in classrooms and automatically relegated to the book sale shelf when donated to public libraries, these books have now become acceptable in both school and public libraries, as well as in classrooms. According to Ed Masessa, the category manager for Scholastic Book Fairs, Bone by Jeff Smith is now one of the hottest titles available at elementary school book fairs around the country. This is especially relevant considering that only about 20 graphic novels (out of the hundreds of thousands of books kids are allowed to self-select off those carts) are available during these book fairs. What's even more impressive is that these 20 titles account for the almost four million graphic novels that have been sold through Scholastic book fairs since the spring of 2004 (Masessa, 2007).

Obviously kids want to read comic books. Your job is to get these books in the hands of eager young readers. My job is to continue to support this movement by writing books to help you make this happen.

I wrote this book because one of the most frequent questions I am asked at workshops around the country is: "What about graphic novels for younger readers?" My hope is that this book will help pick up where my book for preteens and teens left off, providing librarians who serve children and teachers who work with elementary school-aged students with a reputable list of graphic novels that can be added to a library's existing collection. The reason I used the word "comic" in the title instead of "graphic novel" is because I felt like it was a more kid-friendly term.

The intent of this professional resource is to serve as a collection development guide and general reader's advisory tool. The goal of this book is to provide information about developmentally appropriate graphic novels for system-wide selectors, children's librarians, and front line staff in public libraries as well as school library media specialists and teachers working in elementary schools and middle schools. Although many library employees may find the information in this book useful, it will be especially relevant to those who work directly with children between the ages of four and twelve (pre-kindergarten through sixth grade), slightly older reluctant readers in middle school, ESL students, and special needs students. This book is not a comprehensive guide to using the graphic novel format. For that, please see *Getting Graphic! Using Graphic Novels to Promote Literacy with Preteens and Teens*. For more in-depth information about using graphic novels with non-native English speakers, I recommend Stephen Cary's *Going Graphic: Comics at Work in the Multilingual Classroom* (Heinemann 2004).

All of the titles in this book include an annotation, general publication information, companion Web sites where applicable, and a recommended age range. Each age range begins with a recommended low level followed by "and up." This is intentional, as most graphic novels tend to be popular with readers of all ages. A handful of graphic novels in this book are for older, more advanced readers. I have included them because I know there are many elementary students who read on a higher-than-average reading level. These books have exciting plots, well-developed characters, and developmentally appropriate content. However, they do have advanced language, more lengthy passages, and often include text written in a smaller font.

In addition to recommended titles, sample pages from a variety of graphic novels for kids are also included. These illustrations represent the diversity of genres available for younger readers in a comic format, from a fantastic tale about dealing with the beasties in the closet to a surprisingly entertaining nonfiction story about the life cycle of a honeybee. If you are new to the comic format, these illustrations (which have been taken directly from the pages of some of the most popular graphic novels for younger readers) will provide you with an opportunity to experience, firsthand, reading comics created for a new generation of young readers.

This book also includes a list of online resources and professional books about graphic novels in libraries. A glossary is included to help you decipher some of the vocabulary frequently used in the comic publishing industry.

Having said all of that, the main reason I wrote this book is because graphic novels engage readers of all ages. If that's not enough of a reason to include graphic novels in your library's collection, here are ten more reasons why comics for kids are important:

- Graphic novels and comic books offer fast-paced action, conflict, and heroic endeavors—all things young readers embrace.

- Children learn in different ways; visual learners are able to connect with graphic novels and comic books in a way that they cannot with text-only books.

- Graphic novels and comic books require readers to be active participants in the reading process, using their imaginations to fill in the blanks between panels.

- Graphic novels and comic books help young readers develop strong language arts skills including reading comprehension and vocabulary development.

- Graphic novels and comic books contribute to literacy by ensuring that kids continue to read for fun outside of the classroom.

- Graphic novels and comic books often address important developmental assets like being true to yourself, the power of imagination, and teamwork. They also address current, relevant social issues for young readers like divorce, bullying, and the age-old problem of confronting monsters in the closet.

- Graphic novels and comic books provide a perfect bridge for young readers transitioning from picture books to text-only books.

- Graphic novels and comic books often stimulate young readers to branch out and explore other genres of literature including fantasy, science fiction, and realistic fiction as well as nonfiction and myths and legends.

- Graphic novels and comic books are good for ESL (English as a Second Language) students and students who read below grade level because the simple sentences and visual clues allow readers to comprehend some, if not all, of the story.

- Most importantly, graphic novels are a lot of fun and kids enjoy reading them!

COMIC FICTION
FOR YOUNGER READERS

Adventures in Oz (2006)
By Eric Shanower and L. Frank Baum
Publisher: IDW Publishing
ISBN-10: 1933239611; ISBN-13: 978-1933239613

Not surprisingly, there are many graphic adaptations of Frank L. Baum's magical tale about the Land of Oz. This is easily one of the most ambitious versions, coming in at a whopping 250 pages. This mammoth graphic novel is not for everyone, but it's a real jewel for the reader who likes to dive in. Picking up where the movie left off, this story begins when Dorothy returns to Oz to live with the newly throned queen, Ozma. It includes five classic Oz stories: "The Enchanted Apples," "The Secret Island," "The Ice King," "The Forgotten Forest," and the unforgettable "Blue Witch of Oz." Like the story of Oz itself, this book is magical in its telling. This is due in large part to the dramatic, full-color, painted illustrations on every page, but it is also a reflec-

tion of Shanower's attention to detail and faithful adaptation of the classic Oz stories. Grades 5 and up.

The Adventures of Polo (2006)
By Regis Faller
Publisher: Roaring Book Press
IBSN-10: 1596431601; ISBN-13: 978-1596431607;
Polo: The Runaway Book (2007), ISBN-10: 159643189X;
ISBN-13: 978-1596431898

With just his backpack and an umbrella, Polo sets off in his boat on an adventure that will take him on an enchanting journey across the ocean, into the forest, atop an iceberg, up into space, and back home again. This book is reminiscent of *Harold and the Purple Crayon*, if only Harold's imaginary world had been depicted in bold, vibrant colors. In the second volume, Polo's book is captured by a little smiley-faced alien. True to character, Polo sets off after the book and ends up on another journey. Both of these books are

19

Polo: The Runaway Book by Regis Faller

Illustration copyright 2006 Regis Faller from POLO: The Runaway Book, used with permission of Roaring Brook Press.

told entirely in pictures, but the lack of words is really a bonus because it opens the door for a young reader to use his imagination when "reading" Polo's story. This would be great read aloud for storytellers as well as an excellent choice for pre-readers and new readers who are still building their confidence. Grades Pre-K and up.

The Adventures of Tintin

By Hergé
Publisher: Little, Brown Young Readers
Tintin in America / Cigars of the Pharaoh / The Blue Lotus (3 Complete Adventures in 1 Volume, Vol. 1) (1994), ISBN-10: 0316359408; ISBN-13: 978- 0316359405; *The Broken Ear / The Black Island / King Ottokar's Scepte (3 Complete Adventures in 1 Volume, Vol. 2) (1994),* ISBN-10: 0316359424; ISBN-13: 978- 0316359429; *The Crab With the Golden Claws / The Shooting Star / The Secret of the Unicorn (3 Complete Adventures in 1 Volume, Vol. 3) (1994),* ISBN-10: 0316359440; ISBN-13: 978-0316359443; *Red Rackham's Treasure / The Seven Crystal Balls / Prisoners of the Sun (3 Complete Adventures in 1 Volume, Vol. 4) (1995),* ISBN-10: 0316358142; ISBN- 13: 978-0316358149; *Land of Black Gold / Destination Moon / Explorers on the Moon (3 Complete Adventures in 1 Volume, Vol. 5) (1995),* ISBN-10: 0316358169; ISBN-13: 978-0316358163; *The Calculus Affair / The Red Sea Sharks / Tintin in Tibet (3 Complete Adventures in 1 Volume, Vol. 6) (1997),* ISBN-10: 0316357243; ISBN-13: 978-0316357241; *The Castafiore Emerald/ Flight 714/ Tintin and the Picaros (3 Complete Adventures in 1 Volume, Vol. 7) (1997),* ISBN-10: 0316357278; ISBN-13: 978-0316357272

Teenage reporter Tintin and his dog Snowy team up to solve fairly formulaic mysteries, most of which involve criminal mastermind Rastapopoulos and his band of evil henchmen. Originally created in Belgium, Tintin is one of the most popular comics ever to be published in Europe. Although this is not one of those series that will fly off the shelves, it has a proven track record of being a steady circulating title, especially in public libraries where adults often check it out and read it with their children. Grades 4 and up.

Akiko Pocket Size

By Mark Crilley
Publisher: Sirius Entertainment
Volume 1 (2004), ISBN-10: 1579890679; ISBN-13: 978-1579890674; *Volume 2 (2004),* ISBN-10: 1579890687; ISBN-13: 978-1579890681; *Volume 3 (2004),* ISBN-10: 1579890695; ISBN-13: 978-1579890698; *Volume 4 (2006),* ISBN-10: 1579890784; ISBN-13: 978-1579890780; *Volume 5 (2006),* ISBN-10: 1579890792; ISBN-13: 978-1579890797

In this modern day Wizard of Oz, the main character Akiko is a fourth grader who is taken to the planet Smoo. Here she experiences all kinds of adventures, including a sea monster and spy pirates. This series is great for all ages, especially young girls because the main character is a fun and precocious young girl who commands the reader's attention. This series of graphic novels also has a companion series of text-only books for young readers. Graders 4 and up.

Alison Dare: Little Miss Adventures

By J. Torres and J. Bone
Publisher: Oni Press
Volume 1 (2002), ISBN-10: 1929998201; ISBN-13: 978-1929998203; *Volume 2 (2005),* ISBN-10: 1932664254; ISBN-13: 978-1932664256

Alison is not like other girls her age. The daughter of an archaeologist/adventurer and a superhero known as the Blue Scarab, Alison dreams of being anywhere but stuck in the St. Joan of Arc Academy for Girls, where her parents have placed her with the hopes of allowing her to grow up with some semblance of a normal life. Unbeknownst to her parents, Alison and her faithful sidekicks Wendy and Dot have escaped in search of an adventure. Filled with abundant energy, this is one story young readers will adore for its courageous young protagonist and her unlikely escapades. Grades 4 and up.

Amelia Rules!

By Jimmy Gownley
Publisher: Renaissance Press
Volume 1: The Whole World's Crazy (2006), ISBN-10: 0971216924; ISBN-13: 978-0971216921; *Volume 2: What Makes You Happy (2006)*, ISBN-10: 0971216959; ISBN-13: 978-0971216952; *Volume 3: Superheroes (2006)*, ISBN-10: 0971216967, ISBN-13: 978-0971216969; *Volume 4: When the Past is Present (2007)*, ISBN-10: 0971216983; ISBN-13: 978-0971216983

Uprooted from Manhattan and replanted in small-town America, nine-year-old Amelia Louise McBride is just trying to stay afloat and hang on to her sanity after her parents' divorce. In addition to dealing with her parents' breakup, the majority of the first volume is situated around Amelia as she adapts to life in a new town, including making new friends and enrolling in a dreaded new school. In the second volume, Amelia and friends continue their G.A.S.P. (Gathering of Awesome Super Pals) shenanigans, battle the local ninjas, and make a trip to see Amelia's dad in the Big Apple. In Volume 3, Amelia's in for more changes when she moves to a new neighborhood (away from her friends and her favorite rock-n-roller Aunt) and makes a new friend who appears to be hiding a secret. In Volume 4, 11-year-old Amelia is back and better than ever with new adventures including a first "date" and a friend whose dad is being sent to war. Hysterically funny, slightly irreverent, and filled with satirical wit and unexpected wisdom (along with some moments that will pull at your heart strings), this endearing series combines the best of classic comics with a hip new feel for the 21st century. Grades 3 and up.

Artemis Fowl: The Graphic Novel (2007)

By Eoin Colfer, Andrew Donkin, and Giovanni Rigano
Publisher: Hyperion Books for Children
ISBN-10: 0786848812; ISBN-13: 978-0786848812

Twelve-year-old criminal mastermind Artemis Fowl made his fictional debut in 2001. Now he's back and this time young readers can see him in all his scheming and conniving glory illustrated in full-color, in his comic debut, Artemis kidnaps Holly Short, an armed and dangerous fairy captain from the LEPrecon Unit, who does not play by anybody's rules but her own. For readers who are concerned that the graphic novel will not stay true to the original book, creator Eoin Colfer has been quoted as saying, "this is a hundred and twenty pages of sumptuous artwork that sticks very faithfully to the original story." He helped write the adaptation, so I'm sure readers will be pleased. Grades 5 and up.

Avengers and Power Pack Digest Volume 1 (2006)

By Marc Sumerak and Gurihiru
Publisher: Marvel Comics
ISBN-10: 0785121552; ISBN-13: 978-0785121558

The Power Pack is a team of very young superheroes who exist in the Marvel Universe. Consisting of Katie (age 5), Jack (age 8), Julie (age 10), and their leader Alex (age 12), this family of crime fighters team up with well-known superheroes to battle evil, fight for justice, and do good for all mankind—all in time to make it home before bedtime. In Volume I, the Power Pack team up with the Avengers (including Captain America, Spider-Man, Iron Man, and Spider Woman) to battle Kang the Conqueror. For those of you who have graphic novels in your library, you know that superhero titles circulate like crazy. It's nice to see a series (featuring well-known superheroes) that was intentionally written for a younger audience, especially since so many of the superhero comics currently available were written for teens and adults. Grades 3 and up.

Amelia Rules! Volume 3: Superheroes by Jimmy Gownley. Reprinted with permission.

Babymouse

By Matthew Holm and Jennifer L. Holm
Publisher: Random House Children's Books
Our Hero (2005), ISBN-10: 0375832300; ISBN-13: 978-0375832307; *Queen of the World (2005)*, ISBN-10: 0375832297; ISBN-13: 978-0375832291; *Beach Babe (2006)*, ISBN-10: 0375832319; ISBN-13: 978-0375832314; *Rock Star (2006)*, ISBN-10: 0375832327, ISBN-13: 978-0375832321; *Heartbreaker (2006)*, ISBN-10: 0375837981; ISBN-13: 978-0375837982; *Camp Babymouse (2007)*, ISBN-10: 0375839887, ISBN-13: 978-0375839887. *Skater Girl (2007)*, ISBN-10: 0375839895 ISBN-13: 978-0375839894

Spunky, smart, and fueled by a vivid imagination, Babymouse is a dreamer who spends a majority of her time (both in class and out) daydreaming about a glamorous life filled with excitement and adventure! In each of the volumes in this series, Babymouse deals with real-life issues like fitting in with the "popular" crowd, being last chair in the flute section, excelling (okay, maybe not excelling!) in gym class, getting her homework turned in on time, surviving summer vacation with her insufferable family, finding a date for her school's Valentine's Day dance, and making the most of her time at sleepaway camp. All of the books in this endearing series take the young reader inside Babymouse's fantasy world where she really is the smartest, best-dressed, most sought after kid in school, on the beach, and at camp—even if it only lasts until her alarm goes off, the bell rings, or her teacher calls on her for an answer. The simple drawings are fun and reader friendly and the splash of pink throughout each book is sure to be a draw for young girls. This series has an accompanying Web site where kids can create their own Babymouse adventure, find out more about graphic novels and comic books, and play games. This is an ongoing series, so check the Web site for future volumes: <www.babymouse.com>. Grades 2 and up.

The Baby-Sitter's Club

By Ann M. Martin and Raina Telgemeier
Publisher: Scholastic/Graphix
Kristy's Great Idea (2006), ISBN-10: 0439739330; ISBN-13: 978-0439739337; The Truth About Stacey (2006), ISBN-10: 0439739365; ISBN-13: 978-0439739368; Mary Anne Saves the Day (2007), ISBN-10: 0439885167; ISBN-13: 978-0439885164

Since the mid-1980s, books in the Baby-Sitters Club series have been a staple in the lives of young readers. Now these stories are back and better than ever in a comic format, introducing a new generation of kids to the adventures of Stacy, Mary Anne, Kristy, and Claudia—four middle-schoolers who run a profitable after-school business babysitting kids in their neighborhood. In the first volume, the idea for the club is hatched and founding member Kristy gets used to the idea of her mom's remarriage. In Volume 2, the girls deal with a rival babysitter's club and readers find out new club member Stacy is dealing with diabetes. In Volume 3, Mary Anne comes to the rescue of the club by learning to assert herself and playing peacemaker with the group. This series also has a companion Web site where readers can take a quizzes, read sneak peeks of upcoming titles, and find out about the author and illustrator: <http://www.scholastic.com/bscgraphix/>. This series is also ongoing and future volumes are scheduled to be released a couple of times a year. Grades 5 and up.

The Batman Strikes!

By Bill Matheny, Christopher Jones, and Terry Beatty
Publisher: DC Kids
Volume 1: Crime Time (2005), ISBN-10: 1401205097; ISBN-13: 978-1401205096; *Volume 2: In Darkest Night* (2005), ISBN-10: 1401205100; ISBN-13: 978-1401205102.

Like many graphic novel series included in this book, The Batman Strikes! is based on a hit cartoon on the WB network. This is

great news for reluctant readers, especially those who are more interested in flipping channels than pages. Each volume in this series includes five different stories featuring Gotham City's most popular superheroes and villains including Batman, the Joker, Penguin, Catwoman, Mr. Freeze, and more. Grades 3 and up.

A Bit Haywire (2006)
By Scott Zirkel and Courtney Huddleston
Publisher: Viper Comics
ISBN-10: 0977788350; ISBN-13: 978-0977788354

While being chased down an alley by a rabid dog, ten-year-old Owen Bryce takes off running and ends up fifty miles from home, thanks to his newly discovered power of super speed. And this isn't the only superpower that surfaced around the same time; he can fly, he can shoot laser beams out of his eyes, and he can transform into a human torch. This is all great, but there's just one little problem: Owen has no idea how the whole superhero power thing works because his new skills are a little out of whack. Sure he can run super-fast, but only when he holds his breath. He can fly, but only with his eyes closed. Once he discovers his new abilities in the beginning of the story, Owen spends the rest of the book sorting out his new skills, learning about his secret lineage (yep, mom and dad are superheroes), and discovering ways to harness his haywire powers. The cartoony illustrations and bright colors will really pull in readers, especially boys who may not be so keen on the idea of reading. Grades 4 and up.

Bone
By Jeff Smith
Publisher: Scholastic/Graphix
Volume 1: Out From Boneville (2005), ISBN-10: *0439706408; ISBN-13: 978-0439706407; Volume 2: The Great Cow Race (2005),* ISBN-10: 0439706394,

ISBN-13: 978-0439706391; *Volume 3: Eyes of the Storm (2006),* ISBN-10: 0439706386, ISBN-13: 978-0439706384; *Volume 4: The Dragonslayer (2006),* ISBN-10: 0439706378, ISBN-13: 978-0439706377; *Volume 5: Rock Jaw Master of the Eastern Border (2007),* ISBN-10: 043970636X, ISBN-13: 978-0439706360; *Volume 6: Old Man's Cave (2007),* ISBN-10: 0439706351; ISBN-13: 978-0439706353; *Volume 7: Ghost Circles,* ISBN-10: 1888963093; ISBN-13: 978-1888963090; *Volume 8: Treasure Hunters:* scheduled for release in 2008; *Volume 9: Crown Of Horns:* scheduled for release in 2009.

Exiled from Boneville, the three Bone cousins are now lost and separated in the desert by a swarm of locusts. Now good guy Fone Bone, greedy Phoney Bone, and laid back Smiley Bone will have to battle their way back against a legion of evil forces with the help of some unlikely heroes including the mysterious dragon, a seemingly haunted young woman named Thorn, and her Grandma Ben. The well-written dialogue and the interesting plot filled with action and suspense pull the reader in and keep the story line moving throughout the series, but it's Smith's foreshadowing of events to come as well as his completely endearing characters that will keep young readers coming back for more. Filled with intrigue, fantastical elements, a solid cast of unforgettable characters, witty dialogue, and engaging artwork, this is a series that will be a huge hit with fantasy readers who loved the Hobbit but aren't quite ready for the Lord of the Rings. This nine-volume series was originally published in black and white, but each volume is being re-released in color by Scholastic in order to make the series even more appealing to younger readers. For more information about Bone, including a message board, games for kids, character biographies, and an interview with the creator, visit Scholastic's Graphix Web site: <http://www.scholastic.com/bone>. To download "Using Graphic Novels in the Classroom" (a free teacher's guide featuring the characters from Bone) visit Jeff Smith's Web site: <www.boneville.com>. Grades 5 and up.

Bone, Volume 1: Out From Boneville by Jeff Smith. Reprinted with permission.

The Boy, the Bear, the Baron, the Bard (2007)

By Gregory Rogers
Publisher: Roaring Brook Press (March 29, 2007)
ISBN-10: 1596432675; ISBN-13: 978-1596432673

When a little boy kicks his soccer ball into an old, abandoned theater, he is transported back in time to the Globe Theater in London where he comes face to face with a very angry Shakespeare. The boy escapes, only to find himself lost in merry old England during the 16th century. On his journey through the Elizabethan era, the young boy liberates a captive bear, rescues an imprisoned baron from the Tower of London, and runs directly into the path of Queen Elizabeth I. This book exemplifies the concept of a "visual narrative," using only illustrated, sequential panels to convey one boy's adventurous journey through the pages of history. Grades 3 and up.

Buzzboy: Sidekicks Rule! (2007)

By John Gallagher
Publisher: Sky Dog Press
ISBN-10: 0972183175; ISBN-13: 978-0972183178

When Captain Ultra and other superhero members of the Power Coalition are sucked into a mysterious interdimensional vortex, their young sidekicks are left behind to solve the mystery of their disappearance. Unfortunately the second string adult superheroes who are sent in to replace the Power Coalition don't have the skills necessary to keep the planet safe from a host of nefarious villains, much less the time to babysit the sidekicks. Left in the lurch, Captain Ultra's Sidekick Buzz Boy knows that without his superhero mentor he might have to go back to being a normal boy. Knowing that the only thing he ever wanted to be was a superhero, Buzzboy and a few of his underage crime fighting pals will band together to prove that you don't have to be a grown-up to be a hero. This graphic novel also includes drawing tutorials created by popular comic artists and a gallery of superheroes created by young readers to educate and inspire budding cartoonists. Grades 4 and up.

Captain Raptor and the Moon Mystery (2007)

By Kevin O'Malley
Publisher: Walker Books for Young Readers
ISBN-10: 0802796796; ISBN-13: 978-0802796790

Dinosaur heroes, alien invasions, state of the art spaceship, futuristic weapons, underwater adventures with an "octocolossus," the dreaded beast of the sea—all in a comic format with exciting illustrations and great sound effects in giant writing. Really, what more can a young boy want out of a story? Although this looks like a picture book at first glance, it is definitely an oversize science fiction graphic novel intended for younger readers. This is one of those books that will be just as popular for a young child's bedtime story as for a more advanced reader's self-selection. Grades 2 and up.

Carl Barks' Greatest Ducktales Stories

By Carl Barks
Publisher: Gemstone Publishing
Volume 1 (2006), ISBN-10: 1888472367; ISBN-13: 978-1888472363; *Volume 2 (2006)*, ISBN-10: 1888472383; ISBN-13: 978-1888472387

Carl Barks was the legendary cartoonist behind all those classic Disney comics centered around the fictional town of Duckburg, starring Scrooge McDuck, Donald Duck, and the triplets, Huey, Dewey, and Louie, in the 1940s and 1950s. In the late 1980s, many of Barks' stories were adapted for the popular animated cartoon, Duck Tales, drawing a new generation of fans to the franchise. Now the classic comics are back and ready for the next generation of soon-to-be devoted fans in these two collections, each of which includes six of Barks' most popular stories in all their full-color glory. Grades 3 and up.

Comic Zone: Kid Gravity (2006)
Publisher: Disney Press
By Landry Walker and Eric Jones

Kid Gravity is not your average fifth grader—he's the future ruler of the galaxy, and a student at the Hawking School of Astronauts and Astrophysics, an interplanetary boarding school for gifted young students. The mission of the school is to provide young geniuses with both the education and the skills necessary to become either science superheroes or space villains. Other Hawking students include Penny Galactica (a major in cybernetics and advanced robotic engineering), Jetboy and Jetgirl (the snotty twin telepaths who like to finish each other's sentences), "New Kid" (the new alien student from the planet Zarg who is bent on human annihilation), and Kid Apocalypse (Kid Gravity's arch nemesis, who also happens to be his genetically reengineered, evil clone). Each story in this collection (15 in all, averaging between four and nine pages each) centers around some sci-fi concept like time travel, parallel universes, black holes, the second dimension, virtual reality, and more. Coupled with funny dialogue and that age-old battle between good and evil, this graphic novel will be a huge hit with young boys. Grades 3 and up.

The Courageous Princess (2007)
By Rod Espinoza
Publisher: Dark Horse
ISBN-10: 159307719X; ISBN-13: 978-1593077198

Young Princess Mablerose may not be your classic princess, but what she lacks in beauty and grace, she more than makes up for in intellect and resourcefulness. A fairy tale like no other, this is a classic story with a modern twist, in which the young princess rescues herself from the dragon and finds her own way home. This graphic novel is an excellent choice for fans of the fantasy genre who are too young for the more in-depth girl-power stories like those by Robin McKinley and Tamora Pierce. Grades 4 and up.

Fashion Kitty (2005)
By Charise Mericle Harper
Publisher: Hyperion
ISBN-10: 0786851341; ISBN-13: 978-0786851348;
Fashion Kitty versus the Fashion Queen (2007);
ISBN-10: 0786837268; ISBN-13: 978-0786837267

Like Babymouse, Fashion Kitty is a little diva! Unlike Babymouse, Fashion Kitty really is a superhero (instead of just day dreaming about being one) who spends her days fighting for free fashion. What does a fashion superhero do? Well, she has an extraordinary ability to mix and match clothes for those in need, helping the fashion impaired make wise choices about what to wear to be both fashionable and stylistically unique without being a conformist or a fashion faux pas. In Volume 1, Fashion Kitty introduces herself, discovers her secret identity, and helps out a few friends in need of a little fashion guidance. In Volume 2, Fashion Kitty must battle her first evil foe, the spoiled Cassandra, for continued fashion domination of her school. This series is not for everyone, but it will be popular with young girls, especially those who have read all the Babymouse books and are looking for something slightly more difficult—and who have a penchant for all things pink, flowery, and covered in sparkles. Grades 4 and up.

Goosebumps Graphix
By Various Authors
Publisher: Scholastic/Graphix
Volume 1: Creepy Creatures (2006), ISBN-10: 0439841259; ISBN-13: 978-0439841252; *Volume 2: Terror Trips (2007),* ISBN-10: 0439857805; ISBN-13: 978-0439857802 (2007); *Volume 3: Scary Summer (2007),* ISBN-10: 0439857821; ISBN-13: 978-0439857826

Like the Baby-Sitter's Club, Goosebumps is another staple in the massively popular series fiction genre of books for young readers. Providing a new take on an old tale, the three volumes currently available in this newly illustrated series of classic horror stories use creepy (and often stark black

MY PRINCE, HERE I COME!

uhlp!

Oh, WONDERS... SO THAT'S HOW IT FEELS...

ANY MOMENT NOW... HERE COMES MY HANDSOME PRINCE...!

...WHY IS NOTHING HAPPENING?

PARDON ME?

ISN'T THE SPELL BEING BROKEN?

WHAT SPELL?

AREN'T YOU A KIND AND HANDSOME PRINCE CURSED BY AN EVIL WIZARD???

WHY, NO. OF COURSE NOT.

WAHAHA!

148

The Courageous Princess by Rod Espinoza

Text and Illustrations of *Courageous Princess* Copyright 2006 Rod Espinosa, Published by Dark Horse Comics, Inc.

and white) imagery to give these timeless tales an even greater edge. Each volume includes several stories, including "The Abominable Snowman," "The Werewolf of Fever Swamp," and "The Scarecrow Walks at Midnight" in Volume 1; "A Shocker on Shock Street," "One Day at Horrorland," and "Deep Trouble" in Volume 2; and "The Revenge of the Lawn Gnomes" and "The Horror at Camp Jellyjam" in Volume 3. Be warned: the books in this comic series are slightly scarier than their text-only companion novels because of the images. This series also has a companion Web site where kids can create their own comics, read about the authors and illustrators, play games, and talk with other fans on message boards. Librarians can also use this site to find out more about upcoming titles in this ongoing series: <http://www.scholastic.com/goosebumpsgraphix/>. Grades 5 and up.

Grampa & Julie: Shark Hunters (2004)
By Jef Czekaj
Publisher: Top Shelf Productions
ISBN-10: 189183052X; ISBN-13: 978-1891830525

Kids who read Nickelodeon magazine may be familiar with the silly adventures of Grampa and Julie, who have appeared in numerous serialized stories in the magazine over the last few years. In this collected work, Julie's tells her class about how she spent her summer vacation, chasing a shark named Steven with her Grampa. Filled with a lot of silliness and some very outrageous and highly improbable scenarios where Julie and her Grampa battle pirates, befriend a few peanut-butter loving monkeys, engage in a bake-off, capture a rocket ship, win a dance contest, and battle the abominable snowman—all in 65 pages or less! While this is not a book that speaks to adult sensibilities, it is a fun and funny read with color illustrations and a quirky cast of unforgettable characters. Grades 4 and up.

The Hardy Boys
By Scott Lobdell and Daniel Rendon
Publisher: NBM Publishing/Papercutz
#1: The Ocean of Osyria (2005), ISBN-10: 1597070017; ISBN-13: 978-1597070010; #2: Identity Theft (2005), ISBN-10: 1597070033; ISBN-13: 978-1597070034; #3: Mad House (2005), ISBN-10: 1597070106; ISBN-13: 978-1597070102; #4: The Malled (2006), ISBN-10: 1597070149; ISBN-13: 978-1597070140; #5: Sea You, Sea Me! (2006), ISBN-10: 159707022X; ISBN-13: 978-1597070225; #6: Hyde and Shriek (2006), ISBN-10: 1597070289; ISBN-13: 978-1597070287; #7: Opposite Numbers (2006), ISBN-10: 1597070343; ISBN-13: 978-1597070348; #8: Board to Death (2007), ISBN-10: 159707053X; ISBN-13: 978-1597070539; #9: To Die or Not to Die (2007), ISBN-10: 1597070629; ISBN-13: 978-1597070621

Another series of graphic novels based on a classic series of books for young readers, this new generation of Hardy Boys' stories told in a comic format really bring new life to the adventures of boy detectives Frank and Joe Hardy, members of the top-secret ATAC (American Teens Against Crime). Each volume in this series collects multiple stories, although the plot is basically the same in each one: the boy detectives are presented with a mystery and they use their sleuthing skills to uncover the clues that will lead them directly into the heart of the whodunnit. While this is not new fare for the Hardy Boys, these stories have been updated for the 21st century and Frank and Joe solve crimes that reflect today's popular culture, including uncovering who's responsible for a string of identity thefts, who's faking a "reality" TV show for the ratings, who's plotting to kill contestants at a local skateboarding competition, and who's really behind the sky-diving diamond smugglers. Frank and Joe play video games, ride motorcycles, and surf the Internet—all things that obviously never appeared in the classic stories. The illustrations in these books have a very heavy manga influence, which will add to their popularity with younger readers. Grades 5 and up.

Harvey Comics Classics, Volume 1: Casper (2007)

By Leslie Cabarga and Jerry Beck
Publisher: Dark Horse Comics
ISBN-10: 1593077815; ISBN-13: 9781593077815

Everyone's favorite, friendly ghost is back, this time in a collected volume of more than 100 classic stories from the 1950s and 1960s featuring Spooky, Wendy, Nightmare, and the Ghostly Trio. Although the majority of art in this book is black and white, there is a 64-page color section filled with meticulously restored art from the original comics. This old-school style of work will not be popular with everyone, but it will be a favorite for some kids who prefer a sweeter, gentler style that combines fun stories and heartwarming characters. There is also a classic Richie Rich collection of classic comics available from the same publisher. Grades 4 and up.

Herobear and the Kid: The Inheritance (2003)

By Mike Kunkel
Publisher: Astonish Comics
ISBN-10: 0972125914; ISBN-13: 978-0972125918

When Tyler's grandfather passes away, he inherits a stuffed bear and a broken pocket watch. When the watch turns out to be more than what it seems and the outwardly ordinary toy bear comes to life, Tyler's life will never be the same. A timeless tale of friendship, childhood, and heroism, this is the story of a young boy, a magical pocket watch, and a stuffed bear who comes alive to be part of an unlikely, yet loveable, crime-fighting duo. Grades 4 and up.

Hulk and Power Pack: Pack Smash (2007)

By Mark Sumerak
Publisher: Marvel Comics
ISBN-10: 078512490X; ISBN-13: 978-0785124900

The Power Pack is back, and this time they are excited to team up with their father's new colleague, Dr. Bruce Banner. However, the joy is short lived when our team of young superheroes get trapped in a tunnel under New York City with the good doctor because, as you may already know (and our young superheroes are about to find out), when Dr. Banner gets angry, he morphs into the infamous Incredible Hulk. Grades 3 and up.

Jackie and the Shadow Snatcher (2006)

By Lawrence Difiori
Publisher: Knopf Books for Young Readers ISBN-10: 0375875158; ISBN-13: 978-0375875151

Although this book appears to be a picture book at first glance, it is very much a graphic novel for younger readers. Set in the 1920s, this is the story of a young boy named Jackie who has somehow managed to lose his shadow. With the help of his faithful pooch Baxter and the elderly Mr. Socrates, Jackie finds out that the evil Shadow Snatcher (who has escaped from prison and is back to his old tricks) has stolen it from right under his nose. This is one of those classic kid's adventures where the burglars are wearing black stripes and the crime boss uses words and phrases like "scram," "holy mackerel," and "foiled again." It's an easy read and a cute story. Although the black and white pencil drawings in this book may not be all that exciting for some young readers, the illustrations are very clear and provide a lot of context clues to help new readers decipher the text in the word balloons, which are plentiful. Grades 3 and up.

Jetcat Clubhouse (2002)

By Jay Stephens
Publisher: Oni Press
ISBN-10: 1929998309; ISBN-13: 978-1929998302

In the spirit of Spanky and the gang, this story revolves around a group of misfits and their daily happenings in the local clubhouse where a secret password is all you need to be a part of the in-group. Combining juvenile humor and over-the-top slapstick, this graphic novel is both funny and appealing. This story is witty and sometimes even laugh-out-loud funny, full of hilarious superheroes and villains including the title character, elementary student Melanie (a.k.a. Jetcat), her nerdy best friend Tod, Oddette (the richest and hardest rocking child superstar ever), child pharaoh Tutenstein, evil mad genius Bela Kiss, and the irreverent, mischief-making Giant Radio Controlled Robot. It is also well drawn and the short story format really makes this book a good one for struggling readers. Grades 4 and up.

Justice League Unlimited

By Adam Beechen, Carlo Barbieri, Walden Wong, et. al.
Publisher: DC Kids
Volume 1: United They Stand (2005), ISBN-10: 1401205127; ISBN-13: 978-1401205126; Volume 2: World's Greatest Heroes (2006), ISBN-10: 1401210147; ISBN-13: 978-1401210144; Volume 3: Champions of Justice (2006); ISBN-10: 1401210155; ISBN-13: 978-1401210151

Like *The Batman Strikes!*, this series of superhero comics for younger readers is based on an animated television show on the Cartoon Network. Each volume in this series includes five different stories featuring dozens of super-popular superheroes and villains from the DC Universe including Superman, Wonder Woman, the Flash, Green Lantern, and Batman. What's really great about this series is that while it stays true to the original spirit of the League's superheroes (teamwork, truth, trust, and justice), it does not include any of the violence. Grades 3 and up.

King Arthur and the Knights of the Round Table (2007)

Adapted by M.C. Hall, illustrated by C. E. Richards
Publisher: Stone Arch Books
ISBN-10: 1598892185; ISBN-13: 978-1598892185

There are no shortage of books about Camelot and Merlin. The problem is that a lot of these books are really too old for younger elementary students. Taking that into consideration, this is a very good interpretation of the Arthurian legend, especially considering the story is told in 58 pages with very limited text. Although the gist of the story is all there, it has obviously been simplified. The illustrations definitely add to the story, giving young readers a glimpse inside a medieval world filled with wizardry, dragons, castles, and quests. The comic begins with the birth of King Arthur and moves along through his pulling the sword from the stone, his tutelage on how to be a good king under Merlin, his friendship with Lancelot, his marriage to Guinevere, his quest for the Holy Grail, and his final battle with Mordred. This a starter book that will most likely whet the appetite of a child who has a passing interest in classic tales about the Knights of the Round Table. Grades 4 and up.

Korgi, Volume 1: Sprouting Wings (2007)

By Christian Slade
Publisher: Top Shelf Productions
ISBN-10: 1891830902; ISBN-13: 978-1891830907

This is one of those graphic novels that is really hard to describe, but easy to fall in love with after one reading. It's essentially a wordless picture book with a text introduction and character sketches at the end. The core of the story is a beautifully drawn, magical tale about a young girl, her magical dog Sprout, an ogre-type monster, and his minions in the town of Korgi Hollow. It includes a few unexpected plot twists and a very apropos

King Arthur and the Knights of the Round Table adapted by M.C. Hall, illustrated by C.E. Richards. Reprinted with permission.

ending where the monster gets his due. What makes this book really stand out is that all of the illustrations are done using pencil sketches. The creator's attention to detail is phenomenal and his ability to convey the emotions of the dog is genius. This is one of those comics that will not be a favorite for everyone, but the kids who pick it up for the first time and like it will check it out again and again because there is just so much story in these 84 pages. This is an ongoing series, so keep an eye out for future volumes. Grades 3 and up.

Leave it to Chance

By James Robinson and Paul Smith
Publisher: Image Comics
Volume 1: Shaman's Rain (2002), ISBN-10: 1582402531, ISBN-13: 978-1582402536; *Volume 2: Trick or Threat (2003)*, ISBN-10: 1582402787; ISBN-13: 978-1582402789; *Volume 3: Monster Madness (2003)*, ISBN-10: 1582402981; ISBN-13: 978-1582402987

Move over Nancy Drew, fourteen-year-old Chance Falconer has arrived and she is ready to solve a new set of mysteries for a new generation of thriller fans. Born into a

GRAPHIC RESOLVE SERIES

The intended audience for the "Graphic Revolve" series of books is young readers between the ages of 9 and 12, or students in grades 4-6. These books are not intended to replace the originals. Instead, the hope is that they will help developing readers gain an appreciation of the classics so that when they are handed Tom Sawyer or Frankenstein in middle school or high school they not only have a passing familiarity with the story, but a positive connection with these timeless tales of adventure, treachery, and unforgettable characters. Each book in this series features back matter including a glossary, discussion questions, writing prompts, and an author biography. School librarians and teachers will be interested to know that all of the titles in Stone Arch's "Graphic Revolve" series are a part of Accelerated Reader.

Other titles in the series include:

The Adventures of Tom Sawyer (2007)
By Mark Twain, adapted by M.C. Hall, illustrated by Daniel Strickland
ISBN-10: 159889045X; ISBN-13: 978-1598890457

Black Beauty (2007)
By Anna Sewell, adapted by L. L. Owens, illustrated by Jennifer Tanner
Publisher: Stone Arch Books
ISBN-10: 1598890468; ISBN-13: 978-1598890464

Frankenstein (2008)
By Mary Shelley, adapted by Michael Burgan, illustrated by Dennis Calero
ISBN-10: 1598898302; ISBN 13: 9781598898309

H.G. Wells's Time Machine (2008)
By H.G. Wells adapted by Terry Davis, illustrated by Jose Alfonso and Ocampo Ruiz
ISBN-10: 1598898337; ISBN 13: 9781598898330

The Hunchback of Notre Dame (2007)
By Victor Hugo, adapted by L. L. Owens, illustrated by Greg Rebis
ISBN-10: 1598890476; ISBN-13: 978-1598890471

The Invisible Man (2008)
By H.G. Wells, adapted by Terry Davis, illustrated by Dennis Calero
ISBN-10: 1598898310; ISBN 13: 9781598898316

Journey to the Center of the Earth (2008)
By Jules Verne, adapted by David Worth Miller and Katherine McClean Brevard, illustrated by Greg Rebis
ISBN-10: 1598898302; ISBN 13: 9781598898309

Robin Hood (2006)
Adapted by Aaron Shepard and Anne L. Watson, illustrated by Jennifer Tanner
ISBN-10: 1598892193; ISBN-13: 978-1598892192

Treasure Island (2006)
By Robert Louis Stevenson, adapted by Wim Coleman and Pat Perrin, illustrated by Greg Rebis
ISBN-10: 1598890506; ISBN-13: 978-1598890501

family of paranormal investigators, Chance knows she was meant to be part of the family trade. However, her father has different ideas and wants his daughter to live a less dangerous life. But don't worry—this feisty female is too headstrong to take no for an answer. This series is Nancy Drew meets the X-Files and it will most likely appeal to young girls who are not interested in traditional superhero comics. Grades 4 and up.

The Legend of Hong Kil Dong: The Robin Hood of Korea (2006)
By Anne Sibley O'Brien
Publisher: Charlesbridge Publishing
ISBN-10: 1580893023; ISBN-13: 978-1580893022

Although Hong Kil Dong is the son of a powerful minister, his mother is a commoner and therefore he is not entitled to his birthright. It is this injustice that forces Dong to seek out his own destiny on a journey that clearly resembles Robin Hood's quest for justice. This is not the most exciting read, but there are definitely some kids who gravitate to myths and legends who will enjoy this story. Grades 5 and up.

The Life and Times of Scrooge McDuck (2005)
By Don Rosa
Publisher: Gemstone Publishing
ISBN-10: 0911903968; ISBN-13: 978-0911903966; The Life and Times of Scrooge McDuck Companion (2006), ISBN-10: 1888472405; ISBN-13: 978-1888472400

Ever wonder what made Uncle Scrooge so miserly? Creator Don Rosa combed through the classic works of Carl Barks to find the answer to this question, creating twelve excellent stories about what happened to transform Mr. Scrooge from a young duck in Scotland into the richest tightwad in Duckburg. Grades 5 and up.

Lions, Tigers And Bears Volume 1:
Fear And Pride (2006)
By Mike Bullock and Jack Lawrence
Publisher: Image Comics
ISBN-10: 158240657X; ISBN-13: 978-1582406572

When Joey's mom gets a new job, he has to move far away from everything and everyone he knows and loves, including his friends, his newly completed tree house, and his beloved Grandma who lives right next door. Before Joey leaves, Grandma has a surprise for him to help him adjust to his new life: the "Night Pride," a set of four stuffed animals guaranteed to keep him from being lonely in the nighttime. What follows is a classic adventure story where Joey's new stuffed animal protectors come to life to battle the "Beasties" otherwise known as the monsters-in-the-closet in a classic battle that is sure to be one of the biggest in young Joey's life. Like a mix between Calvin and Hobbes and Bedknobs and Broomsticks, this all-ages adventure really is a story about the power of imagination as much as it is about conquering one's fears. Grades 4 and up.

Little Lit
Edited by Art Spiegelman and Françoise Mouly Publisher: Joanna Cotler
ISBN-10: 0060286288; ISBN-13: 978-0060286286; Folklore & Fairy Tale Funnies (2000), ISBN-10: 0060286245; ISBN-13: 978-0060286248; Strange Stories for Strange Kids (2001), ISBN-10: 0060286261; ISBN-13: 978-0060286262; It Was a Dark and Silly Night (2003), ISBN-10: 0060286288; ISBN-13: 978-0060286286; Big Fat Little Lit (Picture Puffin Books, 2006), ISBN-10: 0142407062; ISBN-13: 978-0142407066

All three of these quirky collections of illustrated fables and fractured fairy tales are as off-the-wall as they are imaginative. Edited by Pulitzer Prize-winning author Art Spiegelman and his wife Francois Mouly, the Little Lit series was created with the intention of pulling in a new generation of comic book readers. A majority of the stories in this series

Lions, Tigers, and Bears, Volume 1: Fear and Pride by Mike Bullock and Jack Lawrence. Reprinted with permission.

were written and illustrated by some of the biggest names in the publishing industry, including Lemony Snicket, William Joyce, David Macaulay, Neil Gaiman, and more. Although I recommend purchasing each of the oversized volumes for maximum impact, if your budget is limited, consider adding the new Big Fat Little Lit, a compendium of all the stories, to your collection. The thematic content and artwork in a few stories from each volume is slightly irreverent, so these collections are best suited for more liberal library collections. Grades 5 and up.

Little Lulu Color Special (2006)

By John Stanley and Irving Tripp
Publication: Dark Horse
ISBN-10: 1593076134; ISBN-13: 978-1593076139

Little Lulu made her comic debut in the 1930s. Brought back by Dark Horse Comics for a new generation of readers, Lulu's antics and the funny dialogue in this collection of stories (reproduced in fullcolor for the first time) is sure to win over a new legion of fans. This is one of those books I imagine parents will find reminiscent of their own childhoods and will read aloud with their kids. Grades 3 and up.

Marvel Adventures Fantastic Four

By Various Authors
By Akira Yoshida and Carlo Pagulayan
Publisher: Marvel Comics
Volume 1: Family of Heroes (2006), ISBN-10: 0785118586; ISBN-13: 978-0785118589; Volume 2: Fantastic Voyages (2006), ISBN-10: 0785118594; ISBN-13: 978-0785118596; Volume 3: World's Greatest (2006), ISBN-10: 0785118594; ISBN-13: 978-0785118596; Volume 4: Cosmic Threats (2006), ISBN-10: 0785122087; ISBN-13: 978-0785122081; Volume 5: All 4 One, 4 for All (2007), ISBN-10: 0785122095; ISBN-13: 978-0785122098; Volume 6: Monsters & Mysteries (2007), ISBN-10: 0785123806; ISBN-13: 978-0785123804; Volume 7: The Silver Surfer Digest (2007), ISBN-10: 0785124853; ISBN-13: 978-0785124856

Comics created under the "Marvel Adventures" imprint are intended for a

more about the origin of everybody's favorite wallclimbing superhero. In Volume younger audience, especially children under the age of 12 who want to read superhero comics but aren't quite ready for the language, violence, adult situations, and scantily covered, costumed characters that often appear in many of the comic books written for older audiences. Also, unlike the trade paperbacks that collect the comics written for an older audience, each volume in any "Marvel Adventures" series is a standalone, meaning kids can read them in any order, at any time. This is especially helpful for librarians because it can be difficult to keep the order straight when recommending books in a multi-volume series. Each volume in the "Fantastic Four" series includes four stories featuring Mr. Fantastic, the Invisible Woman, the Human Torch, and the Thing battling bad guys like Dr. Doom, The Incredible Hulk, the Grant Master, and Terminus. Other superhero series published under the "Marvel Adventures" imprint include Spider-Man (see below), Hulk, Iron Man, and The Avengers. Grades 4 and up.

Marvel Adventures Spider-Man

By Various Authors
Publisher: Marvel Comics
Volume 1: The Sinister Six (2005), ISBN-10: 0785117393; ISBN-13: 978-0785117391; Volume 2: Power Struggle (2006), ISBN-10: 0785119035; ISBN-13: 978-0785119036; Volume 3: Doom with a View (2006), ISBN-10: 0785120009; ISBN-13: 978-0785120001; Volume 4: Concrete Jungle (2006), ISBN-10: 078512005X; ISBN-13: 978-0785120056; Volume 5: Monsters on the Prowl (2007), ISBN-10: 0785123091; ISBN-13: 978-0785123095; Volume 6: The Black Costume (2007), ISBN-10: 0785123105; ISBN-13: 978-0785123101; Volume 7: Secret Identity (2007), ISBN-10: 0785123857; ISBN-13: 978-0785123859

This series is an imprint of Marvel Adventures comics (see annotation above), specifically published for younger readers. In Volume 1, Spider-Man faces off with the "Sinister Six," including Mysterio, Vulture, and Sandman. In Volume 2, readers find out more about the origin of everybody's favorite wallclimbing superhero. In Volume 3, Doctor Doom and the Fantastic Four make a guest appearance. In Volume 4, Spidey gets on Aunt May's bad side and must battle it out with the Mad Thinker, the Chameleon, and the Black Cat. In Volume 5, Spider-Man faces a new set of bad guys including Fin Fang Foom and Frankenstein's Monster. In Volume 6, readers will get their first look at Spidey's new "smart stealth" black costume. In Volume 7, Spider-Man battles it out with the Circus of Crime, Night Thrasher, Jester, and the Green Goblin. Other superhero series published under the "Marvel Adventures" imprint include Fantastic Four (see page 20), Hulk, Iron Man, and The Avengers. Grades 4 and up.

The Mighty Skullboy Army Volume 1 (2007)
By Jacob Chabot
Publisher: Dark Horse
ISBN-10: 1593076290; ISBN-13: 978-1593076290

CEO of Skull Company and Commander-in- Chief of the Skullboy Army, young Skullboy is a criminal mastermind and an all-around evil guy. He's also a kid, so instead of running his evil empire he's learning fractions in elementary school. In order to minimize the impact of this time spent in school, Skullboy has recruited two minions to make up the base of his army: Robot (Unit 1), who is loaded down with all kinds of cool gadgets and technology but is really more interested in himself than Skullboy's nefarious schemes and Monkey (Unit 2), a genetically engineered primate who can be really smart at times, but spends most of his time finding ways to amuse himself, thereby wreaking havoc on Skullboy's evil plans. The book is silly, and it's funny, and young boys will love it. Grades 5 and up.

Mouse Guard: Fall 1152 (2007)
By David Petersen.
Publisher: Archaia Studios Press
ISBN-10: 1932386572; ISBN-13: 978-1932386578

The Mouse Guard was formed during medieval times to help protect and defend their own kind from the harsh realities of life outside the burrow, including brutal conditions and an assortment of predators. Members of this elite group are soldiers, sworn to both protect and defend their homestead and act as guides for the mice who need to make the journey from one hidden mouse community to another. They spend their days and nights patrolling the borders and finding safe passages through treacherous territories for members of their extended rodent family. When one of their own goes missing, members of the Guard set out to find him. They discover the cart of the missing mouse merchant, and inside the cart they find plans to their home base. Treason has been carried out, and now they must find the culprit before the predators find them. Look for a second volume soon entitled *Mouse Guard: Winter 1152* in which the mice are back and trying to survive a harsh winter as they struggle to find food and medicine in terrible conditions. This series will be an easy sell for fans of Brian Jacques' *Redwall* series. Mouse Guard is definitely a survival of the fittest story, so there is some violence between the mice and some of their natural predators in these books. Grades 5 and up.

Oddly Normal, Volume 1 by Otis Frampton. Reprinted with permission.

Nancy Drew

By Stefan Petrucha and Sho Murase
Publisher: NBM Publishing/Papercutz
Graphic Novel #1: The Demon of River Heights (2005),
ISBN-10: 1597070009; ISBN-13: 978-1597070003;
Graphic Novel #2: Writ in Stone (2005), ISBN-10:
1597070025; ISBN-13: 978-1597070027; *Graphic
Novel #3: The Haunted Dollhouse (2005),* ISBN-10:
1597070084; ISBN-13: 978-1597070089; *Graphic
Novel #4: The Girl Who Wasn't There (2006),* ISBN-10:
1597070122; ISBN-13: 978-1597070126; *Graphic
Novel #5: The Fake Heir (2006),* ISBN-10:
1597070246; ISBN-13: 978-1597070249; *Graphic
Novel #6: Mr. Cheeters is Missing (2006),* ISBN-10:
1597070319; ISBN-13: 978-1597070317; *Graphic
Novel #7: The Charmed Bracelet (2006),* ISBN-10:
159707036X; ISBN-13: 978-1597070362; *Graphic
Novel #8: Global Warning (2007),* ISBN-10:
1597070513; ISBN-13: 978-1597070515; *Graphic
Novel #9: Ghost in the Machinery (2007),* ISBN-10:
1597070580; ISBN-13: 978-1597070584; *Graphic
Novel #10: The Disoriented Express (2007),* ISBN-10:
1597070661; ISBN-13: 978-1597070669; *Graphic
Novel #11: Monkey-Wrench Blues (2007),* ISBN-10:
1597070769; ISBN-13: 978-1597070768

Everyone's favorite girl detective is back, and this time she's fully illustrated! Nancy Drew has been given a new lease on life in this updated series, and she and her friends George and Bess and her boyfriend Ned are ready to engage in a little undercover sleuthing. Although the stories still have a classic feel, the art has a heavy manga influence that really provides readers with a more contemporary backdrop. The clothes, the haircuts, and even Nancy's vocabulary are more modern, but the stories are still fast-paced and engaging. Readers who might not have picked up a Nancy Drew novel in the past might be inclined to give this new contemporary series a try. Grades 5 and up.

Oddly Normal

By Otis Frampton and Sergio Quijada
Publisher: Viper Comics
Volume 1 (2006), ISBN-10: 097778830X; ISBN-13: 978-0977788309; Volume 2: Family Reunion (2007),
ISBN-10: 0977788393; ISBN-13: 978-0977788392

Ten-year-old Oddly Normal is half witch, half human. Her dad is from Earth, but her mom is from the magical realm of Fignation. Thanks to her mom's genes, Oddly has green hair and pointy ears—physical traits that obviously set her apart from the crowd. An outsider from the beginning, Oddly spends a lot of time in school getting picked on and bullied around. In Volume 1, in a moment of anger and frustration, Oddly wishes her parents would just disappear. When she wakes up, her parents are gone and Oddly has no idea what happened or how to bring them back. Knowing she isn't safe, Oddly's Auntie is sent from Fignation to bring her back for safe keeping. During her time in Fignation, Oddly makes some friends, but she also makes some enemies. In Volume 2, Oddly and her out-of-this world crew (including hunchback Ragnar, Reggie the Frankenstein look-alike, and Oopie, the polymorphic non-biological life form) are teaming up to save Oopie from Ragnar and Reggie's evil father. This series is both smartly written and imaginative, taking ordinary situations like making friends and getting your homework done on time and adding an out-of-this-world twist to pull together one extraordinary reading experience. This is a continuing series. Grades 6 and up.

17

Owly, Volume 3: Flying Lessons by Andy Runton. Reprinted with permission.

Owly

By Andy Runton
Publisher: Top Shelf Productions
Volume 1: The Way Home & The Bittersweet Summer (2004), ISBN-10: 1891830627; ISBN-13: 978-1891830624; Volume 2: Just a Little Bit Blue (2005), ISBN-10: 1891830643; ISBN-13: 978-1891830648; Volume 3: Flying Lessons, ISBN-10: 1891830767; ISBN-13: 978-1891830761; Volume 4: A Time to be Brave (2007), ISBN-10: 1891830899; ISBN-13: 978-1891830891

Owly is a lonely little brown owl who is always on the lookout for new friends. Volume 1 contains two mini-stories. In the first, Owly learns the meaning of friendship when he befriends a little earth worm. In the second, Owly learn that saying goodbye doesn't mean forever when his new hummingbird friends must migrate for the winter. In Volume 2, Owly is determined to befriend a family of bluebirds but the daddy bird wants no part of this unlikely friendship for his family. In Volume 3, Owly is once again on the hunt for new friends and this time he and his friend wormy are determined to befriend the new kid on the block—the flying squirrel. There's just one problem: the flying squirrel only has one natural predator, and it's the brown owl. In Volume 4, Owly and company meet up with a new visitor to the forest who is not what he seems. Although all of these graphic novels are essentially wordless, the artist uses symbols, icons, and pictograms to help tell the story. What really makes these comics stand out from other wordless graphic novels is the incredibly expressive art, which appears relatively simple at first glance. Runton's ability to convey emotion via the animals' facial expressions is remarkable. As readers get older, they will get more out of each story as they begin to comprehend some of the more subtle gestures and facial expressions.
Grades 2 and up.

Pirates of the Caribbean: Dead Man's Chest

(Disney Junior Graphic Novels)
By Stefano Ambrosio and Giovanno Rigano
Publisher: Disney Enterprises
ISBN-10: 142310370X; ISBN-13: 978-1423103707

Jack Sparrow and his crew (including Elizabeth Swann and Will Turner) must battle the treacherous Davy Jones who has come back to redeem a promise Jack made a long time ago. Unlike a lot of graphic adaptations of movies that use screen shots, this is an original comic that was adapted from the screenplay. The art is beautiful and the writing is succinct, but the story remains inclusive of all the things kids love about the orginal story, including action on the high seas, a giant sea beast, and some salty good pirate fun. Other comic adaptations in the Disney Junior Graphic Novels line include *Pirates of the Caribbean: At World's End, The Lion King,* and *Lilo and Stitch.* Grades 4 and up.

Polly and the Pirates (2006)

By Ted Naifeh
Publisher: Oni Press
ISBN-10: 1932664467; ISBN-13: 978-1932664461

Proper young Polly Pringle dreams of an adventurous life on the high seas, gallivanting with pirates and cavorting with Pirate Queen Meg Malloy. Instead, she spends her days under the tutelage of Mistress Lovejoy in a boarding school for girls, where manners, the moral high ground, and practicality reign. But all that is about to change when Polly is shanghaied by a pirate named Scrimshaw who has come looking for a new captain to replace the one who's been gone for a long thirteen years: Captain Meg, Queen of the Pirates . . . and Polly's long lost mother. The pirates need Polly's help to find the map that will lead them back to the Pirate Queen's treasures, but it won't be easy because a rival band of pirates, led by the infamous son of the Pirate King, have also set their sites on the missing booty. When it comes time for Polly to make a

Polly and the Pirates by Ted Naifeh. Reprinted with permission.

choice: the pirate's life or the way of the proper young lady, she lives up to her mom's legacy and comes out with her sword drawn and guns a blazing. This is a great story with a feisty, fearless young heroin and a salty cast of rough but respectful rogues of the sea. This graphic novel does contain quite a bit of saucy pirate language (i.e., sodden 'ell, bloody, daft, etc.) as well as dialogue written in a pirate patois, so it is more suitable for older students. Grades 5 and up.

Power Pack: Pack Attack (2005)
By Mark Sumerak and Gurihiru
Publisher: Marvel Comics
ISBN-10: 0785117369; ISBN-13: 978-0785117360

Every team of superheroes has an origin, and this is the Power Pack's story from the beginning! Alex, Julie, Jack, and Katie Power appear to be pretty normal kids, at first glance. However, these siblings are anything but normal. After an encounter with a dying alien left them with unexplained powers, the foursome agreed to use their powers for good. Like all great superheroes, they transform into villain-fighting good guys when trouble appears. With a simple voice command, they transform into Zero-G, Lightspeed, Mass Master, and Energizer—the youngest team of superheroes in the Marvel Universe. In this introductory volume, the kids battle it out with Larry, the inter-dimensional squid monster, and the dreaded Doctor Doom. Grades 3 and up.

Queen Bee (2005)
By Chynna Clugston-Major
Publisher: Graphix/Scholastic
ISBN-10: 0439715725; ISBN-13: 978-0439715720

Haley and Alexa have the power to rule their middle school, literally! Both girls are psychokinetic, meaning they have the ability to move things with their minds,

but Hayley wants to use her power for good while Alexa has nothing but evil intentions. When the two girls face off in a showdown of power, things are sure to fly! For more information about Queen Bee including class photos, a pop quiz, information about the creator, and a site where pre-teens can send one another e-mail messages, visit Scholastic's Graphix Web site: <http://www.scholastic.com/ queenbee>. Grades 6 and up.

Redwall: The Graphic Novel (2007)
By Brian Jacques, Stuart Moore, and Brett Blevins
Publisher: Philomel
ISBN-10: 0399244816; ISBN-13: 978-0399244810

Some fictional tales really lend themselves to visual storytelling. Redwall is definitely one of those stories, taking the reader along on an epic journey that begins when the peace-loving mice of Redwall Abbey must defend their home from an army of battle-savvy rats led by Cluny the Scourge. In order to defend their home, a young mouse by the name of Matthias will have to embark on a quest to recover the legendary sword of Martin the Warrior in order to protect his community and defeat Cluny and his villainous rodent army. This stand-alone graphic novel is an adaptation of the first novel in the series, so readers do not have to have any prior knowledge of Redwall to really appreciate this book. This classic fantasy series already has a built-in fan base, so this book will most likely circulate heavily among both comic fans and fantasy readers. Grades 5 and up.

Robot Dreams (2007)
By Sara Varon
Publisher: First Second
ISBN-10: 1596431083; ISBN-13: 978-1596431089

A dog goes out and buys a "make your own robot" kit so he can have a friend. After he puts his new robot friend together, Dog and Robot spend all of their time together going

Robot Dreams by Sara Varon

Illustration copyright Sara Varon from *Robot Dreams,* used with permission of First Second Books.

to the library, watching movies, and eating popcorn. Everything is great until Dog and Robot go to the beach, where Robot gets wet and begins to rust. Not aware of how much he has come to love Robot, Dog leaves him behind. The public beach closes for the winter months and Dog must learn to live without his best friend. This is a very simple, very sweet story about friendship. It's entirely wordless, so it's another one of those graphic novels where young readers really have to use their imaginations to tell the story. Grades 4 and up.

Sardine in Outer Space

By Joann Sfar and Emmanuel Guibert
Publisher: First Second
Volume 1 (2006), ISBN-10: 1596431261; ISBN-13: 978-1596431263; *Volume 2 (2006)*, ISBN-10: 159643127X; ISBN-13: 978-1596431270; *Volume 3 (2007)*, ISBN-10: 1596431288, ISBN-13: 978-1596431287; *Volume 4 (2007)*, ISBN-10: 1596431296; ISBN-13: 978-1596431294

This series is for the kid with imagination, the one who dreams about being a pirate (or a space adventurer) and who never met a story he couldn't embellish! Along with the swashbuckling Captain Yellow Shoulder, Sardine and her cousin Little Louise set out to right the wrongs in the galaxy aboard their pirate spaceship, Huckleberry. Their challenge is to bring down out-of-control space tyrant Super-muscleman and his assistant, the Mad Scientist Doc Krok. In Volume 1, readers are introduced to the characters, the mad-cap art with a unique style that is just ugly enough to be cute, and some crazy space menaces and otherworldly creatures. In Volume 2, the gang meets up again with the evil Supermuscleman who has somehow managed to create a brain-washing machine to be used on innocent children. In Volume 3, readers get a ring side seat for the Space Boxing Championship as our quirky cousins go face to face with a

miniature Supermuscleman. In Volume 4, the good guys deal with the monsters under the bed in addition to the traditional evil duo we have all grown to love to hate in the first three volumes. Each volume in this slightly subversive, always quirky, outrageous, and often laugh-out-loud funny series includes twelve individuals stories, which is a great format for the reader with a short attention span or for the kid who just wants a fun and quick read each night before lights out. Grades 4 and up.

Scary Godmother (2005)

By Jill Thompson
Publisher: Sirius Entertainment
ISBN-10: 1579890709; ISBN-13: 978-1579890704

A cross between a comic book and a picture book, Scary Godmother is the story of Hannah Marie and her nasty older cousin Jimmy, who unfortunately has been elected to take her trick-or-treating on Halloween. When Jimmy's plan to frighten his young cousin goes awry, Hannah calls in her own Scary Godmother to protect her while giving Jimmy a taste of his own medicine. A great graphic novel for Halloween, or all year round, young readers will love this kooky, spooky tale about one young girl's liberation from fear. Grades 2 and up.

Shadow Rock (2006)

By Jeremy Love and Robert Love
Publisher: Dark Horse Comics
ISBN-10: 159307347X; ISBN-13: 978-1593073473

After the death of his mom, Timothy is forced to move to the small New England town of Shadow Rock to live with his dad. During the bus ride into town, he finds out that Shadow Rock is considered to be one of the ten most haunted cities in America. When he arrives, Timothy finds out that his new home is right up the hill from a lighthouse, long rumored to be haunted. On his first night in town, Timothy is awakened by a

moaning coming from the lighthouse. A few weeks later, some bullies from school pull a prank on Timothy, leaving him stranded
in the lighthouse alone. Here, he meets the ghost of Kendahl Fog, a young boy who died very mysteriously many years ago. With Kendahl's help, Timothy is determined to find out just how his new friend died. Along the way he will discover some secrets about Shadow Rock that have long been buried. Fans of the Goosebumps series will enjoy this stand-alone story. Grades 4 and up.

Shazam! The Monster Society of Evil (2007)
By Jeff Smith
Publisher: DC Comics
ISBN-10: 1401214665; ISBN-13: 978-1401214661

Shazam! With one word, young Billy Batson can magically transform from a homeless orphan into Captain Marvel, "the world's mightiest mortal," after being granted the power by the great Wizard Shazam. Along with his new powers, his sister Mary (who also has the Shazam! power), and friend Mr. Talky Tawny (who can transform into a tiger), Billy sets out to defeat the evil politician Dr. Sivana and save the world from Mr. Mind and the Monster Society of Evil. Captain Marvel has been around for a long time, but the talent and creativity of Jeff Smith (award-winning creator of the acclaimed "Bone" series) has really breathed new life back into one of the most famous superheroes from the Golden Age of Comics in the 1940s, guaranteeing that a new generation of young fans will be tying on capes and screaming "Shazam!" at the top of their lungs! This title does have some language so it's recommended for more liberal

library collections. Grades 5 and up.

Spider-Man and Power Pack: Big City Superheroes (2007)
By Marc Sumerak and Gurihiru
Publisher: Marvel Comics
ISBN-10: 0785123571; ISBN-13: 978-0785123576

Spider-Man is everybody's favorite nerdy high school student by day and captivating crime-fighting hero by night, so what could be more appropriate than Spidey joining forces with Marvel's youngest team of superheroes, the Power Pack? All four of the stories in this collection are quick and easy reads, making this book a great one to recommend to reluctant readers, especially fans of the Spider-Man movies. Grades 3 and up.

Spiral Bound (2007)
By Aaron Renier
Publisher: Top Shelf Comics
ISBN-10: 1891830503; ISBN-13: 978-1891830501

Turnip, an insecure little elephant, and his friend Stucky Hound embark on an artistic journey in a sculpture class taught by the slightly mysterious Ms. Skrimshaw, a whale from a nearby area called the Pond—a place where no one goes anymore due to some rumors about a nasty monster that inhabits that area. When classmate (and budding reporter) Ana finds out that Ms. Skrimshaw plans to hold the students' sculpture exhibit at the Pond, she releases this information to the community—only to find out too late that putting something in writing can be a very dangerous thing, especially when the facts are not exactly right. Essentially, this is a story about several young, anthropomorphic animal friends who spend their summer exploring possibilities, learning about themselves, realizing their potential, and trying to stay out of both danger and trouble. This book isn't for everyone, but the detailed black and white drawings and the sketchbook feel of the book will be popular with some young readers, especially those kids who are always doodling in their notebooks. Grades 5 and up.

Star Wars: Clone Wars Adventures

By Various Authors
Publisher: Dark Horse Comics
Volume 1 (2004), ISBN-10: 1593075804; ISBN-13: 978-1593075804; *Volume 2 (2004)*, ISBN-10: 1593072716; ISBN-13: 978-1593072711; *Volume 3 (2005)*, ISBN-10: 1593073070; ISBN-13: 978-1593073077; *Volume 4 (2005)*, ISBN-10: 1593074026; ISBN-13: 978-1593074029; *Volume 5 (2006)*, ISBN-10: 1593074832; ISBN-13: 978-1593074838; *Volume 6 (2006)*, ISBN-10: 1593075677; ISBN-13: 978-1593075675; *Volume 7 (2007)*, ISBN-10: 1593076789; ISBN-13: 978-1593076788; *Volume 8 (2007)*, ISBN-10: 1593076800; ISBN-13: 978-1593076801; *Volume 9 (2007)*, ISBN-10: 1593078323; ISBN-13: 978-1593078324

This series focuses on the period of time between two Star Wars movies, the second prequel *(The Attack of the Clones)* and the third prequel *(Revenge of the Sith)*. Each volume contains four short stories that revolve around a war in the Star Wars universe between the Separatist and the Republic. Many popular characters make an appearance in these comics, including Obi-Wan Kenobi, Anakin Skywalker, Darth Sidious, R2-D2, C-3PO, and even the Wookies and Ewoks. This series will circulate heavily among young Star Wars fans. Grades 4 and up.

Sticky Burr: Adventures in Burrwood Forest (2007)

By John Lechner
Publisher: Candlewick
ISBN-10: 0763630543; ISBN-13: 978-0763630546

In Burrwood Forest, a community of seed pods are busy gathering food, building shelter, and getting into all kinds of prickly fun. When Sticky Burr gets stuck in the trunk of a dangerous Maze Tree, his fellow seed pods are getting attacked by dogs in the forest. Can Sticky Burr get away from the tree in time to help his friends? This book is silly, but it's also smart, funny, and very clever. This is quite the feat, considering it's a story that centers around seed pods, otherwise known as burrs. You know, those little things that get stuck all over your socks when you go for a hike in the woods!

Young fans who just can't get enough of Sticky Burr can also go online for more seed pod fun including an ongoing comic strip, games, character sketches, journal entries, and more: <www.stickyburr.com>.

Grades 3 and up.

Stormbreaker: The Graphic Novel (2006)

By Anthony Horowitz, adapted by Antony Johnston, illustrated by Kanako and Yuzuru
Publisher: Philomel
ISBN-10: 0399246339; ISBN-13: 978-0399246333

Fourteen-year-old Alex Rider's life was pretty normal until the day he found out his recently deceased uncle was really a spy for the British government. Now, the same people who employed his uncle have their sights set on Alex as their new boy-wonder super spy. Stormbreaker is Alex's initial journey into a clandestine world filled with intrigue, adventure, danger, and some super cool gadgets that every young reader will covet including zit cream that can melt metal, a backpack parachute, and a Nintendo DS that's really a PDA scanner, transmitter, bug finder, and smoke bomb! Unlike some comic adaptations of text-only books, Alex's introduction to a life of covert operations is actually enhanced by the comic format because the illustrations quicken an already fast-paced plot line. Like the Artemis Fowl adaptation, this is one of those books that will appeal to older elementary school students (especially boys) who have already begun reading higher-level series fiction like the "Alex Rider" series and the "Diamond Brother Mysteries" series by Horowitz or the "Sleeper Code" series by Thomas Sniegoski. Grades 5 and up.

Teen Titans Go!

By J. Torres and Adam Beechen
Publisher: DC Kids
Volume 1: Truth, Justice, Pizza! (2004), ISBN-10: 1401203337; ISBN-13: 978-1401203337; *Volume 2: Heroes on Patrol (2004)*, ISBN-10: 1401203345; ISBN-13: 978-1401203344; *Volume 3: Bring It On! (2005)*, ISBN-10: 1401205119; ISBN-13: 978-1401205119; *Volume 4: Ready for Action (2006)*, ISBN-10: 1401209858; ISBN-13: 978-1401209858

Teenage superheroes' Beast Boy, Cyborg, Raven, Starfire, and Robin (sans Batman) star in this junior version of the Teen Titans. Each volume in this series includes five stories, none of which are dependent on the others so a kid can read any volume, in any order, with just a passing familiarity with the characters. Unlike the *"Teen Titans"* series for older readers, this series is very kid-friendly, with silly plot lines and very little cartoon violence. These books will be especially popular with young readers who are already familiar with the cartoon by the same name. Grades 3 and up.

Tellos: Gargantua (2007)

By Todd Dezago and Mike Wieringo
Publisher: Image Comics
ISBN-10: 1582407894; ISBN-13: 978-1582407890

Fun fantasy for young readers, Tellos is an imaginative mix of myth and legend, bringing together unique characters like the pirate princess and the talking tiger warrior in this exciting adventure that is sure to pull in the most reluctant of readers with dynamic art work and unexpected plot twists. Although the story is relatively simple, the original cast of characters and the fantastic elements make it an interesting read for the most reluctant readers. Grades 4 and up.

Tiger Moth

By Aaron Reynolds and Eric Lervold
Publisher: Stone Arch Books
Insect Ninja (2006), ISBN-10: 1598892282; ISBN-13: 978-1598892284; *Tiger Moth and the Dragon Kite Contest (2006)*, ISBN-10: 1598892290; ISBN-13: 978-1598892291; *The Dung Beetle Bandits (2007)*, ISBN-10: 1598894129; ISBN-13: 978-1598894127; *The Fortune Cookies of Weevil (2007)*, ISBN-10: 1598894137; ISBN-13: 978-1598894134

Young martial arts master and stealth fourth grade ninja, Tiger Moth, uses his skills and abilities to battle evil in the bug world. Along with his ninja apprentice Kung Pow and his friends Slugger and Flutter, Tiger Moth solves crimes and seeks out justice— or at least as much justice as he can seek in between attending Antennae Elementary School and getting his homework done. All of these stories are humorous and there's plenty of language play thanks to a seemingly endless number of puns. Each comic includes information about the author and illustrator, a glossary, a section called "From the Ninja Notebooks," which has all sorts of interesting facts about topics covered in the books, discussion questions, and writing prompts. All are a part of Accelerated Reader. Grades 2 and up.

Time Warp Trio

By Jon Scieszka, adapted by Zachary Rau
Publisher: HarperTrophy
Nightmare on Joe's Street (2006), ISBN-10: 0061116394, ISBN-13: 978-0061116391; *The Seven Blunders of the World (2006)*, ISBN-10: 0061116378; ISBN-13: 978-0061116377; *Plaid to the Bone (2007)*, ISBN-10: 0061116424; ISBN-13: 978-0061116421; *Meet You at Waterloo (2007)*, ISBN-10: 0061116467; ISBN-13: 978-0061116469

Many young readers are familiar with Jon Scieszka's "Time Warp Trio" series in which three young boys travel back in time to experience, firsthand, adventures that happened long ago thanks to a book that was given to one of them as a birthday present. Unlike some books for kids that dumb down the content, the chapter books in the "Time Warp Trio" series are smartly written and funny. The same can be said for the graphic novels, which are fun and engaging with both interesting characters and unique stories that take readers on a journey through space and time with every flip of the page. In Volume 1, the boys are transported back in time to 1816 where Frankenstein is determined to exact revenge against his creator Mary Shelley. In Volume 2, the boys travel back to ancient Babylon where they experience some of the ancient wonders of the world. In Volume 3, the boys travel back to 1338 where they end up in Lady Agnes Randolph's castle in Scotland. In Volume 4 the boys end up in France in 1815 where they are faced with the challenge of making sure Napoleon loses the battle of Waterloo. Although there are only a few volumes available now, with more than 25 episodes of the cartoon I am sure the Time Warp Trio will appear in future graphic adaptations soon. Grades 3 and up.

Tiny Tyrant (2007)
By Lewis Trondheim and Fabrice Parme
Publisher: First Second
ISBN-10: 159643094X; ISBN-13: 978-1596430945

Six year-old King Ethelbert rules the tiny, fictional nation of Portocristo in exactly the way you would expect any spoiled pint-sized monarch to rule: with ridiculous requests, a short temper, and an ego bigger than the country he rules. Ethelbert's outrageous leadership is so over the top that it's funny, demanding to meet Santa Claus, passing new laws that give him absolute authority over all television game shows, and requiring his chef to create a gigantic ice cream sundae, only to take one spoonful before proclaiming he's full. Each of the twelve stories in this full-color collection can stand alone, or be read as a whole. Grades 5 and up.

Twisted Journeys
By Various Authors
Publisher: Graphic Universe
Captured by Pirates (2007), ISBN-10: 0822562022; ISBN-13: 978-0822562023; *Escape from Pyramid X (2007)*, ISBN-10: 0822567792; ISBN-13: 978-0822567790; *Terror on Ghost Mansion (2007)*, ISBN-10: 0822567784; ISBN-13: 978-0822567783; *The Treasure of Mount Fate (2007)*, ISBN-10: 0822562065; ISBN-13: 978-0822562061

We are raising a generation of kids who have grown up with visual, interactive media like computer and video games, games that allow players to make choices and be a part of the story. This is what is great about the "Twisted Journeys" series as a concept. All of the books in this series are choose-your-own-adventure stories in a graphic novel format, providing readers with visual imagery and the opportunity to engage in the story in a meaningful way by making choices at the end of each chapter about what will happen next. Every book has dozens of combinations, so more than one reading is pretty much guaranteed. In Book #1, readers will find themselves in the middle of an adventure on the high seas surrounded by pirates. In Book #2, readers will explore the Egyptian pyramids with the hopes of finding a way to escape the mummies of Pyramid X. In Book #3, readers have to find their way out of a haunted house. In Book #4, readers will test their courage against warriors, wizards, and the dreaded borkadrac! All of the volumes in this series are a part of Accelerated Reader. Grades 4 and up.

Twisted Journeys #2: Escape from Pyramid X by Dan Jolley and Matt Wendt. Reprinted with permission.

W.I.T.C.H.

By Various Authors
Publisher: Hyperion Books for Children/VOLO
Graphic Novel #1: The Power of Friendship (2005),
ISBN-10: 0786836741; ISBN-13: 978-0786836741;
Graphic Novel #2: Meridian Magic (2005), ISBN-10:
0786809744; ISBN-13: 978-0786809745; Graphic
Novel #3: The Revealing (2005), ISBN-10:
0786836555; ISBN-13: 978-0786836550; Graphic
Novel #4: Between Light and Dark (2006), ISBN-10:
0786836563; ISBN-13: 978-0786836567; Graphic
Novel #5: Legends Revealed (2006), ISBN-10:
0786848766; ISBN-13: 978-0786848768; Graphic
Novel #6: Forces of Change (2006), ISBN-10:
0786848774; ISBN-13: 978-0786848775; Graphic
Novel #7: Under Pressure (2007), ISBN-10:
1423106180; ISBN-13: 978-1423106180; Graphic
Novel #8: An Unexpected Return (2007), ISBN-10:
1423109031; ISBN-13: 978-1423109037

Will is new to the town of Heatherfield.
On her first day at the Sheffield Institute,
she is befriended by Irma, Taranee,
Cornelia, and Hay Lin. Within days
strange things begin to happen in town,
including the development of magical
powers by all five girls. The powers use
the four elements of nature (air, earth,
wind, and fire) along with the power of
energy to help the girls do good and battle
evil. Each volume in this series takes the
reader further into the lives of the
W.I.T.C.H. girls as they learn to control
their powers, act as guardians of the Veil,
travel to and from Meridian and the
mysterious realm of Metamoor, and get
themselves into and out of all kinds of
magical trouble. In case that weren't
enough, they have to do all of this while
dealing with the daily pressures of school,
family, and learning to work together as
a team. The W.I.T.C.H. franchise also
includes an animated television show and
a series of text-only chapter books for
younger readers. Grades 5 and up.

The World of Quest (2007)

By Jason T. Kruse
Publisher: Yen Press
ISBN-10: 0759524025; ISBN 13: 978-0-7595-2402-6

In the land of Odyssia, young Prince Nestor
is a real pain. He's spoiled, he's demanding,
and he's a smart aleck. He also happens to
be the only one who knows the whereabouts
of a mystical, magical dagger that holds the
key to the "ultimate power." The problem is
that he cannot go after it alone and so he is
forced to enlist the help of Quest, a reluctant
hero who is not very keen on the idea of act-
ing as a bodyguard for the very ungrateful
Prince. However, by order of the King,
Quest is bound to serve the young noble as
they face off with dangerous bounty hunters
and other evil creatures in order to find the
dagger and rescue the king from the Snarls
and Lord Spite. This is a story with limited
text, but a lot of action that really plays itself
out in vivid colors and a very cartoony,
exaggerated style. This story also has some
really funny dialogue that will appeal to
boys. The World of Quest has also been
adapted into an animated television show
that will debut on the Kids WB in late 2007,
so it will be a good title to entice reluctant
readers. Grades 4 and up.

X-Men and Power Pack, Volume 1:
The Power of X Digest (2006)
By Marc Sumerak and Gurihiru
Publisher: Marvel Comics
ISBN-10: 0785119558; ISBN-13: 978-0785119555

The superhero sibling team is back again and
this time they are joining forces with some of
the world's most famous mutants: Beast,
Cyclops, Nightcrawler,Wolverine, and
Mystique. This graphic novel is an excellent
choice for younger readers who have seen
the X-Men movies, but aren't quite ready for
the X-Men comics created for older teens
and adults. Grades 3 and up.

The World of Quest, Volume I by Jason T. Kruse
From THE WORLD OF QUEST, VOL 1 by Jason Kruse, Copyright 2007 by Jason T. Kruse. By permission of LITTLE BROWN & COMPANY.

MANGA
FOR YOUNGER READERS

What is manga?

The literal translation of the term "manga" is "comic book" in Japanese. Generally rendered in black and white, the art in manga has a very distinct appearance that is often referred to as "manga style."

Some of the more common stylistic elements of manga include simple drawings, characters with large eyes, over-exaggerated emotions, and the use of fewer words to tell the story.

Statistically, manga continues to be one of the fastest growing segments of the graphic novel industry, posting sales in 2006 at an estimated 170-200 million dollars (Griepp, 2007). These numbers do not just reflect manga titles for teen and adult audiences. In fact, two of the top ten manga properties in 2007 were created for younger audiences: Kingdom Hearts and Pokemon (Manga Surge on the Horizon, 2007).

Like graphic novels, manga is a format and not a genre. Like all formats,

manga genres are diverse. The most popular genres of manga include action, romance, sports, mecha (robot stories), drama, horror, science fiction, and comedy.

One of the biggest differences between American comics and Japanese comics are that manga are rated. The major reason for this is because in Japan, manga is read by pretty much everyone, from the business man on the train to the stay-at-home mom to the grandpa who plays Mah Jong in his spare time. Some manga is strictly created for an older teen or more adult audience, and may contain graphic violence, nudity, sex, and adult situations. These books often have a parental advisory label, letting readers know that they are were intended for teens 16 and up or mature adults 18 and up. All of the manga recommended in this book have been rated "A" for all ages or "Y" for youth 10 and up. This introduction to manga is intended to whet your appetite for the format as well as provide you with some beginner guidelines for familiarizing yourself with manga. For more in-depth information about this format, see librarian Robin Brenner's *Understanding Manga and Anime* (Libraries Unlimited, 2007).

Why is manga so popular?

The simple answer: manga is fast paced and emotionally driven. Manga also focuses heavily on character development and it provides American readers with a glimpse inside a culture that is very different from our own. Each volume in a manga series can be compared to a single episode of a television sitcom in that each one tells a piece of the story and it can often take many volumes to complete the story. Again, like a television show, you can read the volumes (or watch the episodes) out of order and you'll get a general idea of the story and characters, but it is only when you sit down and read the series in order (or dutifully watch the show each week) that you begin to develop a vested interest in the characters and the plot line. Unlike traditional American comics (specifically those in the superhero genre), storylines in manga tend to provide readers with more intimate snapshots of daily life. Another big difference between American and Japanese comics is that manga does not always have a happy ending; characters die, lose, and fail. A combination of all of these things is what makes manga so popular, especially with young girls who crave good stories with characters they can hate, love, admire, or with whom they can relate.

Why are these books backwards?

The biggest hurdle for most adults with manga is simply learning to read it. The most important thing to remember about traditional Japanese manga is that it is published as it was intended to be read in Japan and it reads from right to left, back to front. The second most important thing

to understand is that symbols are often used by manga creators to help tell a story, especially when conveying the emotions of a character. Some of the more common symbols (followed by their explanations) include:

- Sweat drops, usually drawn largely on the head region, commonly indicate bewilderment, nervousness, and mental weariness.
- Hatchings on the cheek represent blushing.
- An ellipsis appearing over a character's head indicates an awkward and/or speechless moment.
- Parallel vertical lines with dark shading over the head or under the eye may represent mortification or horror. If the lines are wavy, it may represent disgust.

How do I use the manga section of this book?

The manga in this chapter is sorted into two sub-categories: original Japanese manga and graphic novels created in a "manga style" format.

The first sub-category includes manga created in Japan, translated into English, and published in North America. The majority of the graphic novels in this section will read right to left, back to front (or "backwards" to those of us who have grown up reading books in English). A few of the series in this section do read left to right, front to back, because they were flipped during the translation process.

The second sub-category includes all graphic novels created in a manga-style format that were originally written and published in English. These books read left to right, front to back, like a traditional books written in English. Although these books will likely appeal to manga fans, they are not exactly like traditional manga created in Japan. The biggest difference is that they are more Americanized in both cultural and societal norms.

Original Japanese Manga

All books in this sub-category were originally created in Japan and later translated into English for an American audience. Most books in this section read "backwards," meaning they start at the back of the book and end at the front. The pages are also read from right to left, so a reader starts by reading the comic balloon or text in the top right, then move to the word balloon at the top left. See the illustration "How to Read Manga" for an example about how to read traditional Japanese manga.

B.B. Explosion

By Yasue Imai
Publisher: Viz Media LLC
Volume 1 (2004), ISBN-10: 1591163846; ISBN-13: 978-1591163848; *Volume 2 (2004)*, ISBN-10: 1591163854; ISBN-13: 978-1591163855; *Volume 3 (2004)*, ISBN-10: 1591163862; ISBN-13: 978-1591163862; *Volume 4 (2004)*, ISBN-10: 1591163870; ISBN-13: 978-1591163879; *Volume 5 (2005)*, ISBN-10: 1591163889; ISBN-13: 978-1591163886

Young perfomer Airi dreams about becoming Japan's next rising star. Unfortunately, she lives in Okinanwa Japan, which is a long way from the bright lights of glamorous Tokyo. However, in a stroke of good fortune, Airi is spotted during a local dance competition by a talent scout who believes she really has what it takes to hit the big time. Thanks to her local win, Airi is given the opportunity to attend Actors, a renowned performing arts school in Tokyo. The problem is that her dad has different ideas about her future. Desperate to claim her chance to chase stardom, Airi goes against her father's wishes and moves to Tokyo to hone her performance skills in order to appear on "Boom Boom," an American-Idol type talent contest where young hopefuls compete against one another in the hopes of becoming Japan's next big thing. The competition is fierce, but so is Airi's determination to win over the crowds in order to see her name in lights. This series is classic shojo, brimming with cute characters and an emotional storyline that is very appealing to many young female readers. The focus on the pop-music industry is a good hook, and the plucky young heroine is a refreshing change of pace from the standard action-oriented comic book heroes who normally grace the pages of comics for kids. Grades 5 and up.

Baron the Cat Returns (2005)

By Aoi Hiiragi
Publisher: VIZ Media LLC
ISBN-10: 1591169569; ISBN-13: 978-1591169567

In an act of unanticipated bravery, high-school student Haru rescues a cat from oncoming traffic. Unbeknownst to her at the time, this is not just any cat, but the Prince of the Cat Kingdom. In appreciation, the Cat King summons Haku to his kingdom, where she is informed that she has been deemed the perfect bride for the young Cat Prince. In a desperate attempt to escape the palace and her pending betrothal, Haru seeks out the Baron (a toy cat who has come to life) to help her escape the Cat Palace before it's too late and she is forced to marry into Feline Royalty. In the vein of *Alice in Wonderland,* this is very much a fantasy story about one young girl's adventure into a very alien world where animals talk and things are always more than what they seem. This manga was adapted into a film called *The Cat Returns* a few years ago, so some fans of Japanese animation may already be familiar with the title. Grades 5 and up.

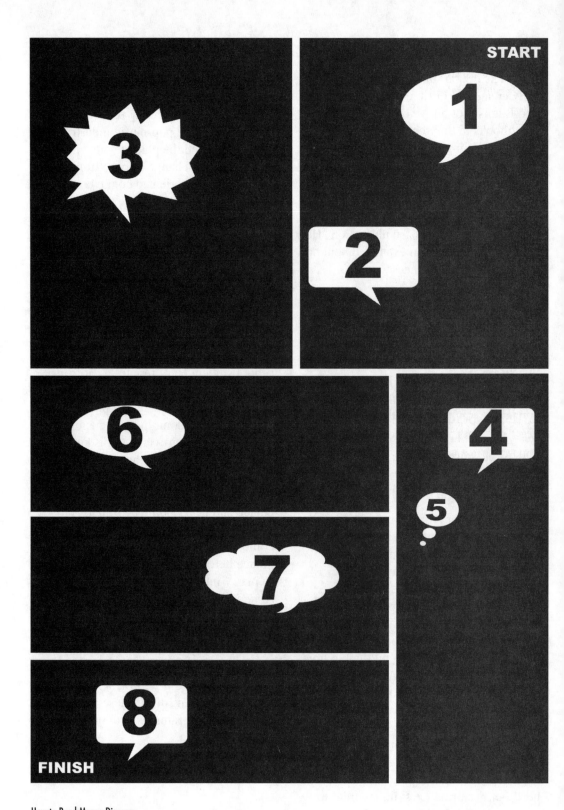

How to Read Manga Diagram.

Beet the Vandel Buster

By Koji Inada and Riku Sanjo
Publisher: Viz Media LLC
Volume 1 (2004), ISBN-10: 159116690X; ISBN-13: 978-1591166900; *Volume 2 (2004)*, ISBN-10: 1591166918; ISBN-13: 978-1591166917; *Volume 3 (2005)*, ISBN-10: 1591166934; ISBN-13: 978-1591166931; *Volume 4 (2005)*, ISBN-10: 1591167507; ISBN-13: 978-1591167501; *Volume 5 (2005)*, ISBN-10: 1591168066; ISBN-13: 978-1591168065; *Volume 6 (2005)*, ISBN-10: 1591168716; ISBN-13: 978-1591168713; Volume 7 (2005), ISBN-10: 1421500760; ISBN-13: 978-1421500768; Volume 8 (2005), ISBN-10: 1421501473; ISBN-13: 978-1421501475; Volume 9 (2006), ISBN-10: 1421502704; ISBN-13: 978-1421502700; Volume 10 (2006), ISBN-10: 1421507714; ISBN-13: 978-1421507712; Volume 11 (2007), ISBN-10: 1421511576; ISBN-13: 978-1421511573; Volume 12 (2007), ISBN-10: 1-4215-1406-0 ; ISBN-13: 978-1-4215-1406-2

This sci-fi/fantasy series takes place in an era known as the "Century of Darkness," where demons with varying degrees of skills and powers (known as Vandels) rule and humans are fearful for their lives. Only one force can stand up to these monsters, and that's the Vandel Busters—a group of trained warriors who use skill and magic to help fight the demons and bring peace back to their world. Main character Beet is a young boy who has his heart set on becoming a Vandel Buster after the Zenon Warriors sacrificed their lives and Saigas (soul weapons) to save him when stumbled into a battle between them and Beltorze the Vandel. Determined to dedicate his life to fulfilling the mission of the Zenon Warriors to end all vandals, Beet enters official training to become a Buster. After three years, Beet has begun to master a few of the Saigas, although he is still learning. Once his training is finished, Beet joins forces with other Busters to annihilate the Vandels in order to avenge the Zenon Warriors and restore his world to one of peace and light. Beet is easily one of the most popular shonen manga series currently available. It does have some fantasy violence, but nothing too explicit. Grades 5 and up.

The Best of Pokemon Adventures

By Hidenori Kusaka and Mato
Publisher: Viz Media LLC
Red (2006), ISBN-10: 1421509288; ISBN-13: 978-1421509280; *Yellow (2006)*, ISBN-10: 142150929; ISBN-13: 978-1421509297

Back in the early 1990s, Pokemon really started the Japanese animation craze in the United States. Now, more than ten years later, Pokemon has made a comeback and has recently surged again in its popularity. Both of these collections contain stories from the "Pokemon Adventures" series; *Red: Volumes 1-3* and *Yellow: Volumes 4-7*. Unlike some of the other books in the Pokemon manga series, both of these collections are based on stories from the video game by the same name. The actual story of Pokemon is difficult to nail down. In *Red*, our young title character is determined to catch the Pokemon. While he is in the process of hunting down the Pokemon, Red finds out some secret information about Team Rocket, who are also hunting down the Pokemon in order to capture and clone Mew—the rarest Pokemon in the world. In *Yellow*, a new kid has arrived in Pallet Town and he's looking for that irresistible electric mouse Pikachu. After befriending Pikachu, Yellow is determined to find Red—the kid who has become to most famous Pokemon trainer of all time. Pokemon was originally published in Japan and later translated into English. Unlike the other traditional Japanese manga titles in this section, both of these books were flipped in translation so they read right to left, front to back, and will therefore be easier for younger readers. Grades 4 and up.

BeyBlade

By Takao Aoki
Publisher: Viz Media LLC
Volume 1 (2004), ISBN-10: 1591166217; ISBN-13: 978-1591166214; *Volume 2 (2004)*, ISBN-10: 1591166977; ISBN-13: 978-1591166979; *Volume 3 (2005)*, ISBN-10: 1591167051; ISBN-13: 978-1591167051; *Volume 4 (2005)*, ISBN-10: 1591167191; ISBN-13: 978-1591167198; *Volume 5 (2005)*, ISBN-10: 1591167930 ; ISBN-13: 978-1591167938; *Volume 6 (2005)*, ISBN-10: 1591168570; ISBN-13: 978-1591168577; *Volume 7 (2005)*, ISBN-10: 1421500191, ISBN-13: 978-1421500195; *Volume 8 (2005)*, ISBN-10: 1421501295; ISBN-13: 978-1421501291; *Volume 9 (2006)*, ISBN-10: 1421502496; ISBN-13: 978-1421502496; *Volume 10 (2006)*, ISBN-10: 1421503808; ISBN-13: 978-1421503806; *Volume 11 (2006)*, ISBN-10: 1421504375; ISBN-13: 978-1421504377; *Volume 12 (2006)*, ISBN-10: 1421504383; ISBN-13: 978-1421504384; *Volume 13 (2006)*, ISBN-10: 1421504391; ISBN-13: 978-1421504391; *Volume 14 (2006)*, ISBN-10: 1421504405; ISBN-13: 978-1421504407

The Bladebreakers are a team of young kids (Tyson, Kai, Ray, and Max) who compete against other teams to win the Beyblading world championship. Their biggest challengers are the Blade Sharks and the Demolition Boys, two teams who will do anything to win—even if it means cheating or stealing powerful Beyblades from another team. A Beyblade is a spinning top enchanted with the spirit of a mythical creature. In battle, two tops charge at one another and creatures called Bit Beasts emerge. If a player has the power to evoke his Bit's special energy, his Beyblade is all the more powerful for it. Beyblade debuted as a manga series in Japan in the late 1990s. At the same time, a series of toys were also introduced. The Beyblade franchise now includes manga, an animated cartoon, a series of toys, a video game, and national and international Beyblade competitions. This series is very popular, especially with young boys. Grades 3 and up.

Cardcaptor Sakura

By CLAMP
Publisher: Tokyopop
Volume 1 (2004), ISBN-10: 1591828783; ISBN-13: 978-1591828785; *Volume 2 (2004)*, ISBN-10: 1591828791; ISBN-13: 978-1591828792; *Volume 3 (2004)*, ISBN-10: 1591828805; ISBN-13: 978-1591828808; *Volume 4 (2005)*, ISBN-10: 1591828813; ISBN-13: 978-1591828815; *Volume 5 (2005)*, ISBN-10: 1591828821; ISBN-13: 978-1591828822; *Volume 6 (2005)*, ISBN-10: 159182883X; ISBN-13: 978-1591828839

Ten-year-old Sakura opens a mysterious book in her father's library. Unbeknownst to her, this book holds the magical clow cards, each of which harbor a powerful ability that can be invoked by wizards, magicians, and card captors to fight the forces of evil. Now that the book has been opened and the cards released, Sakura must recapture them all with the help of Kerberos, the guardian of the Clow Book, before they wreak havoc on the world. It may seem like a simple task, but each one of these cards has its own personality (ranging from fun-loving to extremely mischievous) and the ability to use an alternate form to interact with others. For instance, the Windy Card is one of the four elemental cards. It is very gentle and has the ability to control the winds. The Illusion Card is very aggressive and has the ability to transform itself into whatever the person viewing the card is most afraid of. The Sword Card takes the shape of a sword and it can cut through anything; it also gives the wielder the abilities of a master swordsmen. These cards, along with more than fifteen others, appear in this series. Sakura's job is to capture them all and return them to their rightful place inside the Clow Book. This series has a huge following of preteen and teen girls due in large part to its online presence and popular anime television series. There is also a secondary manga series that picks up where this one ends called "Cardcaptor Sakura: Master of the Clow." This series can be a little confusing due to the premise of the story and the layout of the art and text, so therefore I recommend it for more experienced manga readers. Grades 6 and up.

Di Gi Charat

By Koge Donbo
Publisher: Viz Media LLC
Volume 1 (2003), ISBN-10: 1569319189; ISBN-13: 978-1569319185; *Volume 2 (2003)*, ISBN-10: 156931943X; ISBN-13: 978-1569319437; *Volume 3 (2004)*, ISBN-10: 1591161436; ISBN-13: 978-1591161431; *Volume 4 (2004)*, ISBN-10: 1591161479; ISBN-13: 978-1591161479

Ten-year-old Dejiko is the pampered crown princess of planet Di Gi Charat. She dreams about becoming a superstar but she has to get to Earth first in order for this to happen. The problem when she arrives is that she has no money. So Digiko and friends Puchiko and Gemo get jobs at Gamers, a popular video game store in Japan where they work for minimum wage to pay for food and rent. Someday she'll be crowned the Queen of Di Gi Charact, but for now she just has to find a way to survive Earth and the Dark Gema Gema Gang. The character of Di Gi Charat was originally created as a mascot for an anime and gaming store in Japan. The marketing campaign was so popular that an animated series followed. One potentially confusing element about this series is that each character ends his or her sentences with a particular suffix (Digiko = nya, Puchiko = nyu, Gemo = gema). Although this series is fine for younger readers, older readers will probably have an easier time understanding the speech idiosyncrasies. Grades 6 and up.

Gon

By Masashi Tanaka
Publisher: DC Comics
Volume 1 (2007), ISBN-10: 1401212735; ISBN-13: 978-1401212735; *Volume 2 (2007)*, ISBN-10: 1401212743; ISBN-13: 978-1401212742

Similar to Little Foot in the movie *The Land before Time*, Gon may be tiny but he is a lively and determined little dinosaur who has made it his quest to look out for some of his less adventurous, more easily alarmed friends. Told entirely without words, this is a real visual narrative that makes for imaginative storytelling. More volumes in this series are planned for publication. Grades 3 and up.

Hikaru No Go

Story by Yumi Hotta and Art by Takeshi Obata
Publisher: Viz Media LLC
Volume 1 (2004), ISBN-10: 159116222X; ISBN-13: 978-1591162223; *Volume 2 (2004)*, ISBN-10: 1417734493; ISBN-13: 978-1417734498; *Volume 3 (2005)*, ISBN-10: 1417734507, ISBN-13: 978-1417734504; *Volume 4 (2005)*, ISBN-10: 1591166888 ISBN-13: 978-1591166887; *Volume 5 (2005)*, ISBN-10: 1417734523 ISBN-13: 978-1417734528; *Volume 6 (2006)*, ISBN-10: 1421502755 ISBN-13: 978-1421502755; *Volume 7 (2006)*, ISBN-10: 1421506416 ISBN-13: 978-1421506418; *Volume 8 (2006)*, ISBN-10: 1421506424 ISBN-13: 978-1421506425; *Volume 9 (2007)*, ISBN-10: 1421510669 ISBN-13: 978-1421510668; *Volume 10 (2007)*, ISBN-10: 1421510677 ISBN-13: 978-1421510675

While Hikaru is fooling around in his grandfather's attic, he comes across an old Go board that looks like it has a blood stain on it. He soon finds out that this particular board is haunted by the spirit of Fujiwara no Sai, a fictional Go player from the Heian era in Japan. Sai wishes to play again, but Hikaru has absolutely no interest in playing a game that he considers for old people. But Sai has other plans, and makes Hikaru physically ill until he agrees to play the game for him. He begins by mimicking the

43

Story by Yumi Hotta, art by Obata *HIKARU NO GO* ©1998 by Yumi Hotta, Takeshi Obata/SHLLEISA INC.

moves Sai dictates to him (no one else can see or hear Sai). Although his technique is crude, his play is clearly masterful and those watching do not understand how a kid who has never played before can suddenly beat Akira Toya, a young boy who plays Go at a professional level. What ensues is pretty standard fare: Hikaru finds out he can win money with this gig so he sets out to go pro and win big, all with the help of his magic weapon—Sai. This series is a lot of fun and it takes what could be considered a pretty boring topic of a classic strategy game and turns it into an interesting, action-oriented manga series. Grades 5 and up.

Medabots

By Horumarin
Publisher: Viz Media LLC
Volume 1: A Boy And His 'Bot! (2002), ISBN-10: 1569317720; ISBN-13: 978-1569317723; *Volume 2: Let's Get Ready For Robattle (2002)*, ISBN-10: 1569317739; ISBN-13: 978-1569317730; *Volume 3: The Medaforce (2003)*, ISBN-10: 1569318530; ISBN-13: 978-1569318539; *Volume 4: Finale (2003)*, ISBN-10: 1569318654; ISBN-13: 978-1569318652

Ikki Tenryou wants to win the World Robattle Tournament. Unfortunately, he cannot afford a top-of-the-line Medabot and his parents refuse to buy him one due to the rampant thievery of the popular mini battling robots. As a short-term solution, Ikki manages to scrape together a little money to buy an outdated medabot called a KBT. Then Ikki's dog Salty finds a medal (essentially the medabot's "soul") in the street and when Ikki inserts it into his second rate bot, his KBT instantly transforms into a battle winner. The problem is that the medal Salty found happens to be a rare one that was stolen by the Phantom Renegade. This medal gives Ikki's bot a bad attitude, but he can deal with anything as long as he keeps winning. A cross between Pokemon and Beyblade,

Medabots will most likely appeal to the same audience and will be a good title to recommend when a reader has exhausted all the volumes in those series. Medabots also has an accompanying anime and popular video game. Although this series was originally published in Japan, it was flipped in translation so all volumes read left to right, front to back. Grades 4 and up.

Megaman NT Warrior

By Ryo Takamisaki
Publisher: Viz Media LLC
Volume 1 (2004), ISBN-10: 1591164656; ISBN-13: 978-1591164654; *Volume 2 (2004)*, ISBN-10: 1591164664; ISBN-13: 978-1591164661; *Volume 3 (2004)*, ISBN-10: 1591164141; ISBN-13: 978-1591164142; *Volume 4 (2004)*, ISBN-10: 1591165016; ISBN-13: 978-1591165019; *Volume 5 (2005)*, ISBN-10: 159116561X; ISBN-13: 978-1591165613; *Volume 6 (2005)*, ISBN-10: 1591167558; ISBN-13: 978-1591167556; *Volume 7 (2005)*, ISBN-10: 1421500035; ISBN-13: 978-1421500034; *Volume 8 (2005)*, ISBN-10: 159116981X; ISBN-13: 978-1591169819; *Volume 9 (2005)*, ISBN-10: 1421501325; ISBN-13: 978-1421501321; *Volume 10 (2006)*, ISBN-10: 1421507498; ISBN-13: 978-1421507491; *Volume 11 (2007)*, ISBN-10: 142151141X; ISBN-13: 978-1421511412; *Volume 12 (2007)*, ISBN-10: 1421513250; ISBN-13: 978-1421513256

In the year 200X, everyone is connected to the Cyber Network and computers have helped create a utopian society where there is no war or famine. However, even in an ideal world run by computers, there is bound to be some trouble. A sinister organization by the name of World Threes has vowed to destroy Den Tech City with high-tech crime and computer viruses that will wipe out the entire system, leaving the whole city in ruins. Enter our young protagonist: fifth grader Lan Hikari and his NetNavi, MegaMan. In Den Tech City, every citizen has a PET (Personal Terminal), which is a handheld device that houses a phone, personal computer, and an artificial intelligence program called a NetNavi. A NetNavi acts as a sentient personal assistant who can be "jacked in" to explore the Cyber Network at large. When Lan and his NetNavi MegaMan are synchronized, the two become a power duo—thwarting the World Threes attempts to launch a hostile tech-takeover. This series also has an accompanying anime series, video game, and line of toys. Grades 4 and up.

Tokyo Mew Mew

By Mia Ikumi and Reiko Yoshida
Publisher: Tokyopop
Book 1/Mew Mew to the Rescue (2003), ISBN-10: 159182236X; ISBN-13: 978-1591822363; *Book 2/Three's Company, Five's a Crowd (2003)*, ISBN-10: 1591822378; ISBN-13: 978-1591822370; *Book 3/Party of Five (2003)*, ISBN-10: 1591822386; ISBN-13: 978-1591822387; *Book 4 (2003)*, ISBN-10: 1591822394; ISBN-13: 978-1591822394; *Book 5/The Cat's Out of the Bag! (2004)*, ISBN-10: 1591825482; ISBN-13: 978-1591825487; *Book 6/Blue in the Face! (2004)*, ISBN-10: 1591825490; ISBN-13: 978-1591825494; *Book 7 (2004)*, ISBN-10: 1591825504, ISBN-13: 978-1591825500

The top secret "Mew Project" comes alive when 11-year-old Ichigo and four other pre-teen and teen girls (Mint, Lettuce, Pudding, and Zakuro) are all involved in an accident where each of their DNA is merged with that of an almost extinct animal. Ichigo's DNA is merged with a Irimote Cat, Mint's with the Blue Lorikeet, Lettuce's with the Finless Porpoise, Pudding's with the Golden Lion Tamarin, and Zakuro's with the Gray Wolf. As the girls find one another, their powers get stronger in order for them to defeat the alien force whose mission is to destroy the Earth. This is definitely Shojo manga, and therefore it will be primarily popular with older girls who are already manga readers. It can be a bit confusing at times due to its layout and placement of text on the page, so it's recommended for older readers. Grades 6 and up.

Tokyo Mew Mew a la Mode

By Mia Ikumi and Reiko Yoshida
Publisher: Tokyopop
Volume 1 (2005), ISBN-10: 1595327894; ISBN-13: 978-1595327895; *Volume 2 (2005)*, ISBN-10: 1595327908; ISBN-13: 978-1595327901

Picking up where the original "Tokyo Mew Mew" series left off, the young ladies of the Mew Mew project are back and this time they are searching for a new Mew Mew whose DNA has been merged with not one, but two extinct animals: the Amami Black Rabbit and the Andes Mountain Cat. In this series, the girls will also come face to face with their biggest enemy, a crazy fan who is determined to turn the world against the Mew Mews by releasing subliminal hate messages into the media. There are only two volumes in this follow-up sequel. Grades 6 and up.

Yotsuba&!

By Kiyohiko Azuma
Publisher: ADV Manga
Volume 1 (2005), ISBN-10: 1413903177 ISBN-13: 978-1413903171; *Volume 2 (2005)*, ISBN-10: 1413903185 ISBN-13: 978-1413903188; *Volume 3 (2005)*, ISBN-10: 1413903290 ISBN-13: 978-1413903294; *Volume 4 (2005)*, ISBN-10: 1413903185 ISBN-13: 978-1413903188; *Volume 5 (2007)*, ISBN-10: 1413903495; ISBN-13: 978-1413903492

Little green-haired, five-year-old Yotsuba Koiwai was adopted, but her family and friends aren't really sure where she came from originally. What they do know about her is that she has very little knowledge about everyday things like air conditioning, door bells, escalators, shopping malls, fireworks, and even a swing at the playground. Yotsuba's naivete and quirkiness contribute greatly to the humor in this series. She is also very outspoken and has little use for things like customs and manners. She's adorable and readers of all ages will quickly fall in love with her. Really great comedy manga can be hard to find, especially for

Yotsuba&!, Volume 1 by Kiyohiko Azuma. Reprinted with permission.

younger readers. Yotsuba definitely hits the mark for big laughs. This series really has no plot, just new adventures with Yotsuba in each story. This is great because readers can read them in an order with little or no background knowledge. Grades 5 and up.

Original English Language Manga

A recent trend in publishing graphic novels for younger readers has been to publish original series in a "manga style," meaning they have artistic similarities to traditional manga (especially trim size and black and white art), but they are more Americanized in their content. Unless otherwise noted, all of the books in this sub-category read like traditional English books, beginning in the front, ending in the back, and reading from left to right across the page.

Avatar: The Last Airbender

By Michael Dante Di Martino and Bryan Konietzko
Publisher: TokyoPop
Volume 1 (2006), ISBN-10: 1595328912; ISBN-13: 978-1595328915; *Volume 2 (2006)*, ISBN-10: 1595328920; ISBN-13: 978-1595328922; *Volume 3 (2006)*, ISBN-10: 159816757x; ISBN-13: 978-1598167573; *Volume 4 (2007)*, ISBN-10: 1598169289 ISBN-13: 978-1598169287; *Volume 5 (2007)*, ISBN-10: 1598169297; ISBN-13: 978-1598169294; *Volume 6 (2007)*, ISBN-10: 1598169300; ISBN-13: 978-1598169300

Avatar is set in an Asian-inspired fantasy world where people, mythical creatures, and supernatural spirits coexist. Within this fantasy world, human civilization is divided into four nations: the Earth Kingdom, the Water Tribe, the Air Nomads, and the Fire Nation. Within each nation a group of "benders" have the ability to manipulate (or bend) their elements. This is known as earthbending, waterbending, airbending, and firebending.

However, within each generation, one bender is born who has all four abilities. This person is called the Avatar, and he or she is the manifestation of the planet in human form. The Avatar is born with something called the "Avatar State" and it resides within from birth to death. This power allows the Avatar to possess all the skill and knowledge that have been passed from one generation of Avatar to the next. The Avatar also serves as the bridge between the human world and the spirit world. This series is the story of Aang, a 12-year-old airbender who also happens to be the long-lost Avatar. A century ago, Aang ran away from home to escape the responsibilities of his position. In a freak accident using powers he didn't know he possessed, Aang managed to freeze himself within an air bubble. When he is awakened a hundred years later, he realizes that the four nations have gone to war in his absence and now it is time for him to rise up and acknowledge his birthright and corresponding responsibilities and obligations as the Avatar. *Avatar: The Last Airbender* is a popular cartoon that airs on the Nickelodeon cable television station. Essentially, each volume in this series contains screen shots from the television show along with original dialogue and some interesting layouts and backgrounds. Unlike some comics that only contain screen shots from its companion cartoon, this series is very visually engaging and easy to follow. Volume 1 contains information about the characters and each of the four nations, so readers who are new to the series will be able to follow along without any prior knowledge. Grades 3 and up.

Biker Girl (2006)

By Misako Rocks
Publisher: Hyperion Paperbacks
ISBN-10: 0786836768; ISBN-13: 978-0786836765

When Aki inherits an old bike from her cousin, she acquires more than just a mode of transportation. Upon touching the bike for the first time, Aki suddenly finds herself outfitted in sixties retro biker gear including a very groovy helmet and a pair of old-school goggles. What Aki didn't know before she touched the bike was that in every generation of her family, one must take up the helmet along with the mantel of "bike hero." What she soon finds out is that her cousin Toru was killed on the bike after being run off the road by the leader of a rival biker gang. When Aki is challenged to a race against this same rival, she finds out just how powerful her new bike is, along with learning quite a bit about herself along the way. This book is silly, but in a fun and lighthearted kind of way. Although this book is not traditional manga, the simple art and minimal text will appeal to young manga readers. Grades 5 and up.

Kat & Mouse

By Alex de Campi and Federica Manfredi
Publisher: TokyoPop
Volume 1 (2006), ISBN-10: 1598165488; ISBN-13: 978-1598165487; *Volume 2 (2007)*, ISBN-10: 1598165496; ISBN-13: 978-1598165494; *Volume 3 (2007)*, ISBN-10: 159816550X; ISBN-13: 978-1598165500

When Kat's Dad gets a job teaching science at the prestigious Dover Academy in New Hampshire, Kat and her family move across the country with the hopes of a creating a new life in New England where Kat's mom grew up. Unfortunately for Kat, it's not cool to be the new kid in town—much less the new and unwanted teacher's kid who also happens to be a science wiz. The good news is that Kat has made a new friend—the rebellious computer nerd Mouse. Together the two will take their love of science and computers and team up to help solve mysteries in their school and local community. In Volume 1, one of Kat's dad's students frames him for a crime he didn't commit and it's up to Kat and her new friend Mouse to launch an investigation to find the culprit before Kat's dad loses his job. In Volume 2, Kat and Mouse go on a field trip to the art museum where a famous painting is stolen by a thief known only as the "Artful Dodger." Together, the young detective duo will seek out the guilty party and help restore order (and art) to the museum. In Volume 3, wintertime at Dover Academy means one thing—the Snow Ball, Dover's annual holiday dance. The popular kids are thrilled, but Kat is dreading it because in order to attend she must tutor Chloe (one of the popular girls Kat despises most at her new school) in science. Each volume in this series includes a bonus science experiment that relates to the topic or theme of the story in each book. This is an ongoing series so be sure and look for future volumes at <www.tokyopop.com>. Grades 3 and up.

Kingdom Hearts

By Shiro Amano
Publisher: TokyoPop
Volume 1 (2005), ISBN-10: 1598162179; ISBN-13: 978-1598162172; Volume 2 (2006), ISBN-10: 1598162195; ISBN-13: 978-1598162196; Volume 3 (2006), ISBN-10: 1598166379; ISBN-13: 978-1598166378; Volume 4 (2006), ISBN-10: 1598162209; ISBN-13: 978-1598162202

Amidst a strange storm, 14-year-old Sora is swept from his island home into a strange new land called Traverse Town. At the same time in another world, King Mickey Mouse has disappeared, leaving behind a note for his friends Donald and Goofy instructing them to find the human who holds the key to their survival. Taking their instructions to find the key in Traverse Town, Donald and Goofy set off on their mission to find the key and save their King. Upon arrival, Donald and Goofy come face to face with Sora, who they quickly realize is the holder of the key they are seeking. Together, the threesome will travel by land and sea through many strange lands, searching for clues that they hope will help them find Mickey as well as Sora's friends Kaira and Riku. They must also fight an enemy known as "The Heartless" using Sora's magical Keyblade to seal the keyholes to other worlds to protect them from the strange creatures hunting them down. This best-selling manga series is an adaptation of the extremely popular video game by the same name, so it will likely have a built-in audience. For young readers who are not familiar with the video game, the manga's easily recognizable Disney characters in each volume are sure to be a draw. Older readers are likely to be drawn in by the inclusion of characters from the popular "Final Fantasy" video game. Grades 4 and up.

Kingdom Hearts: Chain of Memories

By Shiro Amano
Publisher: TokyoPop
Volume 1 (2006), ISBN-10: 1598166379; ISBN-13: 978-1598166378; *Volume 2 (2007),* ISBN-10: 1598166387; ISBN-13: 978-1598166385

The sequel to *Kingdom Hearts,* this two-volume manga series continues the story of Sora and friends (including Jiminy Cricket, Donald Duck, and Goofy) as they find themselves investigating the ominous and perilous Castle Oblivion in their continued efforts to try and locate their friends Riku and Mickey Mouse. Unbeknownst to them, Castle Oblivion has the power to make visitors lose their memories, causing the search party many problems as they struggle to remember why they are in this castle in the first place. In addition to this mental duress, the group must also face Organization XIII, the mysterious residents of the castle who have very sinister intentions for Sora and company. Like the first series, these stories are well-written and superbly drawn. Unlike the first series, these two volumes read in a traditional Japanese

manga style of back to front, right to left. Young readers do not have to read the previous story arc in order to understand the story in this series so they can be purchased as a stand-alone series. Grades 4 and up.

Mail Order Ninja

By Erich Owen and Joshua Elder
Publisher: TokyoPop
Volume 1 (2006), ISBN-10: 1598167286; ISBN-13: 978-1598167283; Volume 2 (2006), ISBN-10: 1598167294; ISBN-13: 978-1598167290; Volume 3 (2007), ISBN-10: 1598167308; ISBN-13: 978-1598167306

Bully magnet Timmy McAllister spends the majority of his day at school getting picked on and pushed around, so when he reads an advertisement in a catalog announcing "The Great Ninja Warrior Gunshyo Giveaway" he has nothing to lose by entering to win his own personal ninja. A few weeks later, Timmy's ninja Yoshida Jiro arrives in a packing crate. At first his parents are totally against him having a ninja because, after all, owning a ninja is a big responsibility. However, with a little pleading and some big promises to always feed and water his new friend, Timmy is finally granted permission to keep his new ninja. What happens next is every misfit's dream come true: ninja fighting the bad guys at school, ninja demonstrating his master techniques during show-and-tell, ninja teaching martial arts during gym, boy (no longer misfit) winning student council election thanks to popularity of new ninja sidekick. In addition to this series being a lot of fun, the writing is witty and the artwork is outstanding. This is an ongoing series so be sure and look for future volumes at <www.tokyopop.com>. Grades 4 and up.

Mail Order Ninja, Volume 1 by Joshua Elder and Erich Owen

New Alice in Wonderland Color Manga (2006)

By Lewis Carroll and Rod Espinosa
Publisher: Antarctic Press
ISBN-10: 0976804387, ISBN-13: 978-0976804383

Like Baum's Land of Oz, there have been many adaptations of Lewis Carroll's time-less tale about Alice's fall down a rabbit hole and chance encounter with the unfor-gettable, fantastical White Rabbit, the Duchess, and the Mad Hatter. Although this is not one of the most exciting adapta-tions of this classic story, Espinoza's stylistic manga rendition is sure to pull in voracious manga readers who are looking for something new. Grades 5 and up.

Neotopia Color Manga

By Rod Espinoza
Publisher: Antarctic Press
Volume 1 (2004), ISBN-10: 1932453571; ISBN-13: 978-1932453577; *Volume 2 (2004)*, ISBN-10: 193245358X ISBN-13: 978-1932453584; *Volume 3 (2005)*, ISBN-10: 193245375X ISBN-13: 978-1932453751; *Volume 4 (2005)*, ISBN-10: 1932453857 ISBN-13: 978-1932453850

Neotopia is set in the land of Mathenia, a utopian society a thousand years in the future where creatures of myth and magic have returned to live in harmony with the humans now that that the world is no longer ruled by greed, industrial pollution, and technological excess. This four-volume series centers around feisty Nayla, an abused servant posing as the Grand Duchess in the absence of her boss, royal daughter Nydia. In direct contrast to Nydia, Nayla is good, true, and loyal. Her inner circle is composed of Ki-Ek, an intelligent and specially gifted dolphin who can speak; Nimn, an elf who uses his magic to harness mystic ways (as well as turn servant Nayla into the beautiful but cruel Nydia); Marro, an orphaned elf trained by humans to serve and protect the royal family as a member of the BodyGuard Elite; Professor Felder, who is

responsible for Nayla's education, and Philios, a young inventor, expert float ship mechanic, and Airdiver apprentice. Together this cast of unlikely heroes will defend Mathenia in an all-out battle between good and evil when the dark empire of Krossos attempts to steal the Grand Duchess, ignit-ing a war that will last throughout the four-volume series. A solid cast of characters, beautiful and majestic artwork, and imagi-native storytelling all contribute to a well-rounded story that will be a hit for manga readers as well as more traditional sci-fi/fantasy crossover readers. Unlike traditional manga, all illustrations in this series are full-color. This is a very text-heavy series (written in a small font), so that may deter some readers. Grades 5 and up.

Oz: The Manga, Pocket Manga Volume 1 (2006)

By David Hutchison
Publisher: Antarctic Press
ISBN-10: 1932453695; ISBN-13: 978-1932453690

Recreated through the lens of Japanese comics, this visually appealing, manga-style adaptation of Frank L. Baum's timeless tale is sure to be hit with both fans of the original story and new readers who have no idea that the movie was actually based on a book! Unlike the movie, this faithful retelling does a great job of providing readers with more of the back story about the Scarecrow, the Tin Man, and the Cowardly Lion. Grades 5 and up.

Peach Fuzz

By Lindsay Cibos and Jared Hodges
Publisher: Tokyopop
Volume 1 (2005), ISBN-10: 1595325999 ISBN-13: 978-1595325990; Volume 2 (2006), ISBN-10: 1595326006 ISBN-13: 978-1595326003

Nine-year-old Amanda thinks the solution to her loneliness is a new pet, but when her new ferret Peach shows her true nature as a biter, Amanda has to find a way to keep this information hidden. If her mom finds out that her new furry friend has some violent tendencies, she will have to return him to the pet store. This clever new manga series was the first ever to be syndicated in American newspapers, so many young readers may have a passing familiarity with it. This is an ongoing series, so be sure and look for future volumes at <www.tokyopop.com>. Grades 4 and up.

Sonic the Hedgehog, Archives

By Mike Gallagher and Dave Manak
Publisher: Archie Comic Publications
Volume 1 (2006), ISBN-10: 1879794209 ISBN-13: 978-1879794207; Volume 2 (2006), ISBN-10: 1879794217 ISBN-13: 978-1879794214; Volume 3 (2007), ISBN-10: 1879794225 ISBN-13: 978-1879794221; Volume 4 (2007), ISBN-10: 1879794241 ISBN-13: 978-1879794245; Volume 5 (2007), ISBN-10: 1879794268 ISBN-13: 978-1879794269; Volume 6 (2007), ISBN-10: 1879794276 ISBN-13: 978-1879794276

Sega's mascot Sonic the Hedgehog (a.k.a. the Blue Blur) made his debut in videogames in 1991. In 1993 Sonic made his inaugural appearance in a comic book. In 2008, Sonic and Archie Comics are celebrating their 15th anniversary in comicdom by re-releasing the original stories created during the last decade and a half in these new archives, which feature the first 24 comic book issues starring Sonic, Miles "Tails" Prower, Shadow the Hedgehog, Knuckles the Echidna, Amy

Rose and other characters who populate Planet Mobius in Knothole Kingdom. Sonic has also appeared in his own hit cartoon, so most young readers are familiar with him from either playing the video game or watching the television show. The popularity of the title character is what will move this book off the shelves continuously. It also helps that the books are small in both trim size and page length (each one contains four issues and each issue includes two mini-stories), the art is bright and very cartoony, and there is a lot of action on every page. Grades 4 and up.

Warriors

By Erin Hunter, Dan Jolley, and James Barry
Publisher: TokyoPop
Volume 1, the Lost Warrior (2007), ISBN-10: 0061240206; ISBN-13: 978-0061240201; Volume 2, Warrior's Refuge (2007), ISBN-10: 006125231X; ISBN-13: 978-0061252310; Volume 3: Warrior's Return (2007), ISBN-10: 0061252336; ISBN-13: 978-0061252334

This graphic novel series is based on the popular juvenile fantasy "Warriors" series. The general premise of the text-only novels is that four clans (ThunderClan, ShadowClan, RiverClan, and WindClan) of feral cats have escaped domestication and must fight to stay alive in the wilderness, all the while obeying the laws laid down by their feline warrior ancestors. The graphic novel adaptation of this acclaimed series is actually a new story about one of the Warrior's most beloved feline heroes— Graystripe. In what is essentially a backstory, readers find out more about Graystripe's life with the humans (a.k.a. "twolegs") and his escape and reunion with the ThunderClan. The manga trilogy basically bridges the gap between "The New Prophecy" series and the "Power of Three" series, and although readers do not have to have read any of the Warriors novels to really enjoy the comics, it is helpful. This comic trilogy will likely pull

Warriors, Volume 1: The Lost Warrior by Erin Hunter, Dan Jolley. Reprinted with permission.

in readers who are not traditional fans of comics and graphic novels because *Warriors* fans will want to read about Graystripe's past. Grades 4 and up.

Zapt!

By Armand Villavert, Shannon Denton, and Keith Giffen
Publisher: TokyoPop
Volume 1 (2006), ISBN-10: 1598165887 ISBN-13: 978-1598165883; *Volume 2 (2007),* ISBN-10: 1598165895 ISBN-13: 978-1598165890

Welcome to the world of Armad Jones, a kid from Earth who has just been abducted by the Panagalactic Order of Police (more commonly known as P.O.O.P.) to be one of their newest operatives. After a tough initiation, Armad and his new best friend Payleen (a member of the loathsome alien Panadekian race) are sent out to protect the Galaxy. Unfortunately, things go wrong from the very start for these two misfits. First they are captured by Space Pirates. Then they find themselves personally responsible for rescuing an alien princess from the evil Gongar and his loyal servant Terros, an ex-P.O.O.P. operative who just happens to have been one of the best agents, ever! This comic will definitely appeal to boys who dream of adventure and high jinks among the stars. This is an ongoing series so be sure and look for future volumes at <www.tokyopop.com>. Grades 3 and up.

COMIC NONFICTION FOR YOUNGER READERS

Alia's Mission: Saving the Books of Iraq (2004)
by Mark Alan Stamaty
Publisher: Knopf Books for Young Readers
ISBN-10: 0375832173; ISBN-13: 978-0375832178

Iraqi librarian Alia Muhammed Baker rescued 30,000 books from the central library in Basra before Iraq was invaded by hostile forces in 2003. Determined to protect the library's collection, which she considered a record of her country's history and culture, Baker took on the dangerous task of physically moving thousands of volumes from the library to safe places throughout the community. Inspired by a true story, this graphic novel is a thoughtful account about the impact of war on civilians. Stamaty, a wellknown cartoonist for the *New York Times Book Review*, really captured the heart of this story in the details, using art to help deliver a very powerful read without being overly political. Although the illustrations are all done in black and white, the action in the illustrations and the intensity of the story

are likely to pull in young readers who may have little or no information about the war in Iraq outside of what they have seen on television. Grades 5 and up.

Amaterasu: Return of the Sun (2007)
By Paul D. Storrie and Ron Randall
Publisher: Lerner Publishing Group
ISBN-10: 0822559684; ISBN-13: 978-0822559689

This graphic novel tells about the Japanese myth of Amaterasu, the Shinto Goddess of the Sun. Amaterasu and her seven brothers and sisters were born to God and Goddess Izanagi and Izanami. They represented the first eight islands of Japan and were each responsible for a portion of the earth, including the sun and sky and the seas and storms. Benelovent Amaterasu lived in the Heavens and ruled the sun. Unfortunately, her brother Susano had been given responsibility for the seas and storms, and he was jealous of his sister's position. In fear of her brother, Amaterasu goes

Amaterasu: Return of the Sun: A Japanese Myth by Paul D. Storrie and Ron Randall. Reprinted with permission.

into hiding—thereby causing darkness to fall upon her people. In order to lure their sister from the cave and restore light to their country, Amaterasu's brothers and sisters seek out the wisdom of Omohi-kane for his help devising a clever ruse to help draw their sister from the darkness. In the end, the ruse works, light is restored, and the evil Susano is banished to the underworld. It's an interesting story and one that will be unfamiliar to a lot of kids. The front matter includes facts about the first eight islands of Japan and an accompanying map. A simple introduction to the Shinto religion and the shrine of Amaterasu is also included, in addition to a very basic description about how people in Japan continue to worship her today. Back matter includes a glossary and pronunciation guide, index, further reading and Web sites about Japan's Gods, Goddesses, and native religion Shinto. Grades 5 and up.

GRAPHIC UNIVERSE: GRAPHIC MYTHS AND LEGENDS SERIES

The intended audience for Lerner's "Graphic Universe: Graphic Myths and Legends" series is young readers between the ages of nine and twelve, or students in grades four through six. Each book in this series features back matter including sources notes that provide details about the origin of each legend, information about how the writer and illustrator did research for each particular book, relevant maps, a glossary, further reading, and an index. You can buy each title in paperback for a fraction of what you would pay for a library bound hardcover. If you are not sure how these books will circulate, give them a trial run with paperback copies. Something else that really sets the books in this series apart from some of the other graphic novels focusing on myths and legends is that they are all written, illustrated, and produced by professionals in the comic publishing industry. Also, all of the books in this series are a part of Accelerated Reader.

Other titles in the series include:

Arthur & Lancelot: the Fight for Camelot (2007)
By Jeff Limke and Thomas Yeates
ISBN-10: 0822562960; ISBN-13: 978-0822562962

Atalanta: The Race Against Destiny (2007)
By Justine Fontes, Ron Fontes, and Thomas Yeates
ISBN-10: 082255965X; ISBN-13: 978-0822559658

Beowulf: Monster Slayer (2007)
By Paul D. Storrie and Ron Randall
ISBN-10: 0822567571; ISBN-13: 978-0822567578

Demeter & Persephone: Spring Held Hostage (2007)
By Steve Kurth and Barbara Schultz
ISBN-10: 0822559668; ISBN-13: 978-0822559665

Hercules: the Twelve Labors (2007)
By Paul D. Storrie and Steve Kurth
ISBN-10: 0822564858; ISBN-13: 978-0822564850

Isis & Osiris: To the Ends of the Earth (2007)
By Jeff Limke and David Witt
ISBN-10: 0822564823; ISBN-13: 978-0822564829

Jason: Quest for the Golden Fleece (2005)
By James Riordan and Jason Cockcroft
ISBN-10: 1845070615; ISBN-13: 978-1845070618

King Arthur: Excalibur Unsheathed (2007)
By Jeff Limke and Thomas Yeates
ISBN-10: 0822564831; ISBN-13: 978-0822564836

Odysseus: Escaping Poseidon's Curse (2007)
By Dan Jolley and Thomas Yeates
ISBN-10: 0822562081; ISBN-13: 978-0822562085

Robin Hood: Outlaw of Sherwood Forest (2007)
By Paul D. Storrie and Thomas Yeates
ISBN-10: 0822559641; ISBN-13: 978-0822559641

Sinbad: Sailing into Peril (2007)
By Marie P. Croall and Clint Hilinski
ISBN-10: 0822563754; ISBN-13: 978-0822563754

Theseus: Battling the Minotaur (2007)
By Jeff Limke and John McCrea
ISBN-10: 0822567563; ISBN-13: 978-0822567561

Thor & Loki: In the Land of Giants (2006)
By Jeff Limke and Ron Randall
ISBN-10: 0822530872; ISBN-13: 978-0822530879

The Trojan Horse: The Fall of Troy (2007)
By Ron Fontes, Justine Fontes, and Gordon Purcell
ISBN-10: 082256484X; ISBN-13: 978-0822564843

Yu the Great: Conquering the Flood
By Paul D. Storrie and Sandy Carruthers
ISBN-10: 0822530880; ISBN-13: 978-0822530886

AT 12:00 P.M., CAMERAMAN JOE ROSENTHAL TOOK THE MOST FAMOUS PHOTO OF THE WAR AS A SECOND, LARGER FLAG WAS RAISED TO REPLACE THE FIRST FLAG.

OF THE SIX MARINES WHO RAISED THE SECOND FLAG, ONLY THREE SURVIVED THE BATTLE.

ONE OF THE SURVIVORS WAS IRA HAYES, A NATIVE AMERICAN OF THE PIMA TRIBE FROM ARIZONA.

A TRIBAL ELDER HAD TOLD HAYES WHAT IT MEANT TO BE AN HONORABLE WARRIOR.

FIGHT BRAVELY. KILL IF YOU MUST, BUT TAKE NO PRIDE IN IT. IF YOU RETURN, WE WILL KNOW YOUR DEEDS. NEVER BOAST OF WHAT YOU DID IN WAR.

THE FLAG-RAISING PHOTO MADE IRA HAYES A NATIONAL HERO. HE WAS SENT AROUND THE COUNTRY ON A TOUR TO SELL WAR BONDS.

HE WASN'T BOASTING HIMSELF, BUT IT WAS ALL THE SAME TO HIS TRIBE. HE HAD BROKEN ONE OF ITS MAJOR TABOOS.

21

The Battle of Iwo Jima: Guerilla Warfare in the Pacific by Larry Hama and Anthony Williams. Reprinted with permission.

Amelia Earhart: Free in the Skies (2003)

By Robert Burleigh
Publisher: Silver Whistle Books
ISBN-10: 0152168109; ISBN-13: 978-0152168100

This illustrated biography for younger readers highlights a handful of historical moments in Earhart's life, from her first ride in a plane to her first solo flight across the Atlantic. The downside of this biography is that it does not include a bibliography or cited resources. However, it can serve as high-interest, supplemental reading material for a child doing a research project on Amelia Earhart. Grades 3 and up.

The Battle of Iwo Jima: Guerrilla Warfare in the Pacific (2007)

By Larry Hama and Anthony Williams
Publisher: Rosen Publishing Group
ISBN-10: 1404207813; ISBN-13: 978-1404207813

This book has a couple of great strengths. The first is that the author does a really good job of showing both the American and Japanese military (foot soldiers and commanders) as real people, staying true to the facts and leaving out general opinions and hypothetical language. The second is that all factual information appears in yellow text boxes. Narrative fiction (of which there is very little) appears in white word balloons. Finally, the detailed descriptions of weapons and guerilla warfare tactics used by both countries to try and outlast one another will really engage reluctant readers. By all accounts, the Battle of Iwo Jima during World War II was one of the bloodiest battles in American history. In spite of that, the depiction of war in this graphic novel is relatively tame in comparison to a lot of books about warfare intended for older audiences. The camouflaged art shows action, but no gratuitous violence. In fact, there is no blood splatter in this entire book. Other than the fact that the author did not include citations for direct quotations, this is a fine book in a very engaging series that will be a natural fit for young readers who have an interest in historical military combat. Front matter includes five pages of text about the beginning of World War II, information about key commanders in this war, and the role the small island of Iwo Jima played in this battle. A few photos and map of Iwo Jima are also included. Back matter consists of a text-only passage about the United States' road to victory against Japan as well as a few photos, an extensive glossary, further reading, and an index. Grades 5 and up.

This graphic novel is one of several historical nonfiction titles in Rosen's "Graphic Battles of World War II" series.

GRAPHIC BATTLES OF WORLD WAR II

The intended audience for Rosen's "Graphic Battles of World War II" series is older elementary school students and middle school students. Although the subject of this series is war, the depiction of war is not overtly graphic in these books. There is very little information on these topics in a graphic novel format for younger readers, and the general subject of war is one that will pull in reluctant readers. Each book in this series includes a glossary, contact information for organizations related to the topic of the book, further reading, and an index. All six of the titles in the "Graphic Battles of World War II" series are a part of Accelerated Reader. Rosen Publishing also has another graphic novel series focusing on battles of the Civil War that may be of interest to older students who enjoy the books in this series.

Other titles in the series include:

The Battle of the Bulge: Turning Back Hitler's Final Push (2007)
By Doug Murray
ISBN-10: 1404207821 ISBN-13: 978-1404207820

The Battle of Guadalcanal: Land and Sea Warfare in the South Pacific (2007)
By Larry Hima
ISBN-10: 1404207848; ISBN-13: 978-1404207844

continued on page 62

The Battle of Midway: The Destruction of the Japanese Fleet (2007)
By Steve White
ISBN-10: 140420783X; ISBN-13: 978-1404207837

D-Day: The Liberation of Europe Begins (2007)
By Doug Murray
ISBN-10: 1404207864; ISBN-13: 978-1404207868

Pearl Harbor: A Day of Infamy (2007)
By Steve White
ISBN-10: 1404207856; ISBN-13: 978-1404207851

Clan Apis (2000)

By Jay Hosler
Publisher: Active Synapse
ISBN-10: 096772550X; ISBN-13: 978-0967725505

An illustrated biography of a honeybee named Nyuki, this graphic novel is an original and creative combination of scientific detail and in-depth black and white illustrations describing the life cycle and natural environment of the honeybee. While the life of a honeybee may not seem to be an interesting topic at first glance, this book really brings the concept to life for young readers who have an interest in the natural sciences. Grades 6 and up.

Drawing Comics is Easy, Except When It's Hard (2006)

By Alexa S. Kitchen
Publisher: Denis Kitchen Publishing Company
ISBN-10: 097100806X; ISBN-13: 978-0971008069

This book was created by America's youngest cartoonist, seven-year-old Alexa Kitchen. Daughter of cartoonist Denis Kitchen, Alexa definitely inherited the drawing gene from her dad. This how-to book is both informative and entertaining and it includes advice, samples, and step-by-step instructions for drawing faces, portraying emotions, and creating costumes. Alexa also gives some great for advice for other budding artists. This book is an excellent motivational tool for all those kids out there who want to be professional artists. Although kids of all ages will enjoy this book, the majority of the text is in Alexa's handwriting, which might make it difficult for younger readers to decipher. Grades 4 and up.

Into the Air: The Story of the Wright Brothers' First Flight (2002)

By Robert Burleigh and Bill Wylie
Publisher: Silver Whistle Books
ISBN-10: 0152024921; ISBN-13: 978-0152024925

This is the story of Orville and Wilbur Wright told in a comic book format. The story begins with the Wright's bike shop in Dayton, Ohio and takes the reader along as the brothers begin designing and testing flying machines. It includes information about their historical first flight in Kitty Hawk, North Carolina in 1903 and it ends with them continuing to dream up new and exciting ways to take to the air. The book has a lot of cheesy fictional dialogue that can be somewhat disruptive, but other than that it is a decent bibliography that will be of interest to younger readers who are having a hard time working their way through a text-only nonfiction title about the first brothers of flight. Like the Amelia Earhart biography, this book does not include a bibliography or cite any resources. It is best for pleasure reading or supplemental reading material for a biography assignment. Grades 3 and up.

Satchel Paige: Striking Out Jim Crow (2007)

By James Sturm and Rich Tommaso
Publisher: Hyperion Books for Children
ISBN-10: 0786839007; ISBN-13: 978-0786839001

Narrated by fictional Alabama sharecropper (and former baseball player in the Negro Leagues) Emmet Wilson, this graphic novel is

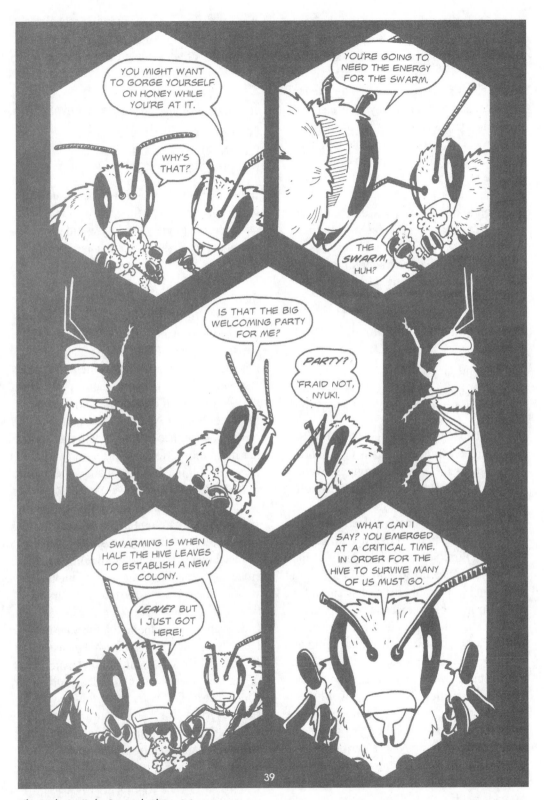

Clan Apis by Jay Hosler. Reprinted with permission.

as much a story about the racial divide in the segregated American South as it is about Baseball Hall-of-Famer Leroy "Satchel" Paige's pitching career that spanned five decades. It's a historical look at the Negro Leagues, and in a lot of ways it is a story about the "Great American Dream." Paige was a real character and a storyteller, and all of this is reflected in the pages of this graphic novel, published in collaboration with the Center for Cartoon Studies. The attention to detail, solid artwork, and pacing all contribute to a very engaging graphic biography that sports fans will enjoy as well as more traditional readers looking for a solid piece of storytelling. Grades 5 and up.

The Strongest Man in the World: Louis Cyr (2007)

By Nicholas Debon
Publisher: Groundwood Books
ISBN-10: 0888997310; ISBN-13: 978-0888997319

Set in Quebec Canada in the early 1900s, this is French-Canadian Louis Cyr's auto-biography as the World's Strongest Man. The story begins with Cyr letting his young daughter Emiliana know that during a recent medical physical his doctor told him that continuing in his profession would likely kill him. So on this, the night of his last performance for the circus carrying out seemingly impossible feats of strength for his adoring public under the big top, Cyr recounts his life for his daughter beginning with how he got started, his upbringing and training, and his exploits using his strength to woo the crowds for years as a performer in a traveling circus. In the afterword the reader finds out that some of the records Cyr set more than a hundred years ago remain unbroken today. The earth-toned paintings in this graphic novel are very subdued, so this book will not likely appeal to readers who are looking for the flashier, brighter comics. However, the story is interesting and it will appeal to a small percentage of young readers, especially

those who have an interest in sports and those who are looking for a biography of an athlete. Grades 3 and up.

To Dance: A Ballerina's Graphic Novel (2006)

By Sienna Cherson Siegel and Mark Siegel
Publisher: Atheneum/Richard Jackson Books
ISBN-10: 0689867476; ISBN-13: 978-0689867477

In her first autobiographical graphic novel, writer Siena Cherson Siegel takes the reader along on her journey into the world of profes-sional ballet. Beginning at the age of six, Siena took lessons in Puerto Rico. When her family moved to Boston a few years later, Siena continued her lessons and it was during this period of her life that she saw a perform-ance of the Bolshoi Ballet starring the great Russian prima ballerina, Maya Plisetskaya. Plisetskaya's performance as the dying swan cemented Siena's desire to dance profession-ally. At the age of eleven, Siena auditioned for the School of American Ballet in New York City. Her acceptance meant that she and her mom moved to New York, away from her dad who still lived in San Juan. Once enrolled in SAB, Siena became aware of the hard work, long hours, dedication, and sacrifices a young dancer had to make in order to be good enough to dance professionally. The rest of the chapters tell about some of the mile-stones in Siena's life as a dancer, including wearing toe shoes, performing for the first time, dancing at Lincoln Center, surviving adolescence including her parent's divorce, letting go of her beloved dance teacher Mr. B., and finally sustaining an injury at the age of eighteen that put an end to her professional dance career. This story is touching, with sparse, lyrical prose, and beautiful illustrations created by Siena's husband Mark Siegel. Although it may seem strange to have a graphic novel about ballet, the comic format was an excellent choice for this story because it really pulls the reader in and takes her along on the journey of one young girl's dream. Grades 4 and up.

To Dance: A Ballerina's Graphic Novel by Siena Cherson Siegel and Mark Siegel. Reprinted with permission.

UFOs: The Roswell Incident (2007)

By Jack DeMolay
Publisher: PowerKids Press
ISBN-10: 1404221565; ISBN-13: 978-1404221567

Cashing in on the unexplained, this graphic novel addresses what really happened in Roswell, New Mexico in

JR. GRAPHIC MYSTERIES SERIES

The intended audience for Rosen's Jr. Graphic Mysteries series is young readers between the ages of eight and twelve, or students in grades three through six. Each graphic novel addresses some unknown phenomena, famous mystery, or unexplained theory, and all are spooky but not scary. All titles are 24 pages and feature back matter including a glossary and pronunciation guide. All six titles in this series are a part of Accelerated Reader.

Other titles in the series include:

Atlantis: The Mystery of the Lost City (2007)
By Jack DeMolay and Q2a
ISBN-10: 1404221603; ISBN-13: 978-1404221604

The Bermuda Triangle: The Disappearance of Flight 19 (2006)
By Jack DeMolay
ISBN-10: 1404234047; ISBN-13: 978-1404234048

Bigfoot: A North American Legend (2006)
By Jack DeMolay
ISBN-10: 1404234055; ISBN-13: 978-1404234055

Ghosts of Amityville: The Haunted House (2007)
By Michael Marts and Jack DeMolay
ISBN-10: 1404221557; ISBN-13: 978-1404221550

The Loch Ness Monster: Scotland's Mystery Beast (2006)
By Jack DeMolay
ISBN-10: 1404234063; ISBN-13: 978-1404234062

1947 and tries to answer the questions about this alien mystery that some claim is a cover up. There are a lot of books about this for older readers, but very few for a younger audience. The full-color illustrations and large text make this an easy read and the subject makes it both interesting and engaging for even the most reluctant readers. Grades 3 and up.

Capstone Graphic Library

We all know that series nonfiction books are not the most exciting books in the library. Unfortunately, these are the books that are most often pulled off the shelves when elementary students have to give a report or complete an assignment about a historical event or famous person. More often than not, when a student comes in asking for these books, the librarian is left scrambling to find something on the shelves that looks remotely interesting while at the same time covers the basic information the student needs for his homework. Taking this into consideration, Capstone launched a series of high-interest, nonfiction graphic novels for younger readers that cover a variety of subjects and themes, including biographies, historical events, principles of science, disasters in history, and inventions and discoveries.

All of the graphic novels in Capstone's Graphic Library have a professional consultant or expert in the particular field or topic covered in each book. Each 32-page graphic novel contains a table of contents and direct quotations that appear in yellow word balloons so young readers know this information was taken from primary sources. Fictional dialogue appears in white word balloons and narration appears in gray text boxes. Each book also contains additional back matter including more information about the book's subject (presented as "factoids" in a bulleted list), a "Read More" section with other recommended books about the subject, a glossary, a bibliography, recommended Web sites (which lead the young reader to Facthound (<www.facthound.com>, a somewhat useful Web portal that provides readers with links to Web sites that are both safe and easy to navigate when they plug in their book's ISBN or general subject), and an index. Additionally, each title includes developmentally appropriate educational content aligned to national curriculum standards. All of the titles in Capstone's Graphic Library are a part of Accelerated Reader. These books will never win any awards for their art or prose, but they do provide a young reader with a decent amount of information in a high-interest format. All of these series are ongoing, so visit Capstone's Web site for information about new titles each season: <www.capstonepress.com>.

Capstone Graphic Library: Graphic Biographies Series

Mother Jones: Labor Leader (2006)

By Connie Colwell Miller, Steve Erwin, and Charles Barnett III
Publisher: Capstone Press
ISBN-10: 0736896627; ISBN-13: 978-0736896627

Mary Harris was born in Ireland in the 1840s, around the time of the great potato famine that left many Irish farmers with no way to make a living. In the 1850s, Mary's family moved to Toronto, Canada with the hope of being able to find work. Some time

n the next decade Mary moved to Memphis, Tennessee where she met and married George Jones and settled down to raise a family. However, the couple had a hard time financially because this was in the middle of the Industrial Revolution, when people were losing employment opportunities to machines. All around her, Mary saw people losing their jobs and being forced into poverty. In 1867, Yellow Fever struck Memphis, killing Mary's husband and children. In order to get away from her loss, she moved to Chicago where she was once again surrounded by terrible working conditions, overworked and under paid workers, under age child laborers, and unsafe labor practices. In the late 1890s, Mary became an organizer for the United Mine Workers. She spent the next few years uniting the miners and helping them rise up against unfair work practices. During this period of time Mary earned the nickname "Mother" because she treated the mine workers like family. She went on to help the coal miners, factory workers, and children laborers— going as far as to march on Washington and serve time behind bars for her role as an advocate for enslaved laborers and a pioneer for the labor movement as a whole. In a lot of ways this graphic novel is basically an illustrated encyclopedia entry, but it will definitely be more interesting for a struggling reader who might be more inclined to cut and paste from Google than to actually read a print biography. Grades 4 and up.

Capstone's "Graphic Library: Graphic Biographies" series also include the following books:

Amelia Earhart: Legendary Aviator (2007)
By Jameson Anderson
ISBN-10: 0-7368-6496-2; ISBN-13: 9780736864961

Benedict Arnold (2007)
By Michael Burgan
ISBN-10: 0-7368-6854-2; ISBN-13: 9780736868549

Benjamin Franklin: An American Genius (2006)
By Kay Melchisedech Olson
ISBN-10: 0-7368-4629-8; ISBN-13: 9780736846295

Bessie Coleman (2007)
By Trina Robbins
ISBN-10: 0-7368-6851-8; ISBN-13: 9780736868518

Booker T. Washington: Great American Educator (2006)
By Eric Braun
ISBN-10: 0-7368-4630-1; ISBN-13: 9780736846301

continued on page 68

Cesar Chavez: Fighting for Farmworkers (2006)
By Eric Braun
ISBN-10: 0-7368-4631-X; ISBN-13: 9780736846318

Christopher Columbus (2007)
By Mary Dodson Wade
ISBN-10: 0-7368-6853-4l ISBN-13: 9780736868532

Clara Barton: Angel of the Battlefield (2006)
By Allison Lassieur
ISBN-10: 0-7368-4632-8; ISBN-13: 9780736846325

Eleanor Roosevelt: First Lady of the World (2006)
By Ryan Jacobson
ISBN-10: 0-7368-4969-6; ISBN-13: 9780736849692

Elizabeth Blackwell: America's First Woman Doctor (2007)
By Trina Robbins
ISBN-10: 0-7368-6497-0; ISBN-13: 9780736864978

Elizabeth Cady Stanton: Women's Rights Pioneer (2006)
By Connie Colwell Miller
ISBN-10: 0-7368-4971-8; ISBN-13: 9780736849715

Florence Nightingale (2007)
By Trina Robbins
ISBN-13: 9780736868501; ISBN-10: 0-7368-6850-X

George Washington Carver: Ingenious Inventor (2006)
By Nathan Olson
ISBN-13: 9780736854849; ISBN-10: 0-7368-5484-3

George Washington: Leading a New Nation (2007)
By Matt Doeden
ISBN-10: 0-7368-4963-7; ISBN-13: 9780736849630

Helen Keller: Courageous Advocate (2006)
By Scott Welvaert
ISBN-10: 0-7368-4964-5; ISBN-13: 9780736849647

Jackie Robinson: Baseball's Great Pioneer (2006)
By Bob Lentz
ISBN-10: 0-7368-4633-6; ISBN-13: 9780736846332

Jane Goodall: Animal Scientist (2006)
By Katherine E. Khron
ISBN-13: 0-7368-5485-1; ISBN-10: 9780736854856

Jim Thorpe: Greatest Athlete in the World (2008)
By Jennifer Fandel
ISBN-10: 1-4296-0152-3; ISBN-13: 9781429601528

John F. Kennedy (2007)
By Nathan Olson
ISBN-10: 0-7368-6852-6; ISBN-13: 9780736868525

Martin Luther King Jr.: Great Civil Rights Leader (2007)
By Jennifer Fandel
ISBN-10: 0-7368-6498-9; ISBN-13: 9780736864985

Matthew Henson: Artic Adventurer (2006)
By B.A. Hoena
ISBN-10: 0-7368-4634-4; ISBN-13: 9780736846349

Molly Pitcher: Young American Patriot (2006)
By Jason Glaser
ISBN-13: 9780736854863; ISBN-10: 0-7368-5486-X

Muhammad Ali: American Champion (2008)
By Michael Burgan
ISBN-10: 1-4296-0153-1; ISBN-13: 9781429601535

Nathan Hale: Revolutionary Spy (2006)
By Nathan Olson
ISBN-13: 0-7368-4968-8; ISBN-10: 9780736849685

Patrick Henry: Liberty or Death (2006)
By Jason Glaser
ISBN-13: 9780736849708; ISBN-10: 0-7368-4970-X

Sacagawea: Journey into the West (2007)
By Jessica Gunderson
ISBN-10: 0-7368-6499-7; ISBN-13: 9780736864992

Samuel Adams: Patriot and Statesman (2007)
By Matt Doeden
ISBN-10: 0-7368-6500-4; ISBN-13: 9780736865005

Theodore Roosevelt (2007)
By Nathan Olson
ISBN-10: 0-7368-6849-6; ISBN-13: 9780736868495

Thomas Jefferson: Great American (2006)
By Matt Doeden
ISBN-10: 0-7368-5488-6; ISBN-13: 9780736854887

William Penn: Founder of Pennsylvania
By Ryan Jacobson
ISBN-10: 0-7368-6501-2; ISBN-13: 9780736865012

Wilma Rudolph: Olympic Track Star
By Lee Engfer
ISBN-10: 0-7368-5489-4; ISBN-13: 9780736854894

Many of Capstone's Graphic Biography (Biografías Gráficas) titles are also available in Spanish. These include:

Benjamin Franklin: un genio norteamericano (Benjamin Franklin: An American Genius) (2007)
By Kay Melchisedech Olson
Publisher: Capstone Press
ISBN-10: 0-7368-6598-5; ISBN-13: 9780736865982

Booker T. Washington: gran educador norteamericano (Booker T. Washington: Great American Educator) (2007)
By Eric Braun
Publisher: Capstone Press
ISBN-10: 0-7368-6599-3; ISBN-13: 9780736865999

Cesar Chavez: lucha por los trabajadores del campo (Cesar Chavez: Fighting for Farmworkers) (2007)
By Eric Braun
Publisher: Capstone Press
ISBN-10: 0-7368-6600-0; ISBN-13: 9780736866002

Clara Barton: Angel del campo de batalla (Clara Barton: Angel of the Battlefield) (2007)
By Allison Lassieur
Publisher: Capstone Press
ISBN-10: 0-7368-6601-9; ISBN-13: 9780736866019

Eleanor Roosevelt: primera dama del mundo (Eleanor Roosevelt: First Lady of the World) (2007)
By Ryan Jacobson
Publisher: Capstone Press
ISBN-10: 0-7368-6607-8; ISBN-13: 9780736866071

Elizabeth Cady Stanton: pionera de los derechos de las mujeres (Elizabeth Cady Stanton: Women's Rights Pioneer) (2007)
By Connie Colwell Miller
Publisher: Capstone Press
ISBN-10: 0-7368-6609-4; ISBN-13: 9780736866095

George Washington: dirigiendo una nueva nacion (George Washington: Leading a New Nation) (2007)
By Matt Doeden
Publisher: Capstone Press
ISBN-10: 0-7368-6605-1; ISBN-13: 9780736866057

Helen Keller: valiente defensora (Helen Keller: Courageous Advocate) (2007)
By Scott Welvaert
Publisher: Capstone Press
ISBN-10: 0-7368-6604-3; ISBN-13: 9780736866040

Jackie Robinson: gran pionero del beisbol (Jackie Robinson: Baseball's Great Pioneer) (2007)
By Jason Glaser
Publisher: Capstone Press
ISBN-10: 0-7368-6602-7; ISBN-13: 9780736866026

Matthew Henson: aventurero del Artico (Matthew Henson: Arctic Adventurer) (2007)
By B.A. Hoena
Publisher: Capstone Press
ISBN-13: 9780736866033; ISBN-10: 0-7368-6603-5

Nathan Hale: espia revolucionario (Nathan Hale: Revolutionary Spy) (2007)
By Nathan Holsen
Publisher: Capstone Press
ISBN-10: 0-7368-6606-X; ISBN-13: 9780736866064

Patrick Henry: muerte o libertad (Patrick Henry: Liberty or Death) (2007)
By Jason Glaser
Publisher: Capstone Press
ISBN-10: 0-7368-6608-6; ISBN-13: 9780736866088

Capstone Graphic Library: Graphic History Series

The First Moon Landing (2007)

By Thomas K. Adamson and Gordon Purcell
ISBN-13: 9780736864923; ISBN-10: 0-7368-6492-X

This graphic novel provides young readers with a glimpse inside what happened before, during, and after our country's first journey to the moon, including a glimpse at the rivalry between the USA and the Soviet Union. Although this graphic novel does not provide a wealth of information about the birth of NASA or any information about our country's existing space program, it does provide basic information about the early years of the USA's space exploration program. Grades 4 and up.

 Capstone's "Graphic Library: Graphic History" series also include the following books:

The Adventures of Marco Polo (2005)
By Roger Smalley
ISBN-10 : 0-7368-3830-9; ISBN-13: 9780736838306

The Assassination of Abraham Lincoln (2005)
By Kay Melchisedech Olson
ISBN-10: 0-7368-3831-7; ISBN-13:9780736838313

The Battle of Gettysburg (2006)
By Michael Burgan
ISBN-10: 0-7368-5491-6; ISBN-13: 9780736854917

The Battle of the Alamo (2005)
By Matt Doeden
ISBN-10: 0-7368-3832-5; ISBN-13: 9780736838320

Betsy Ross and the American Flag (2006)
By Kay Melchisedech Olson
ISBN-10: 0-7368-4962-9; ISBN-13: 9780736849623

The Boston Massacre (2006)
By Michael Burgan
ISBN-10: 0-7368-4368-X; ISBN-13: 9780736843683

The Boston Tea Party (2005)
By Matt Doeden
ISBN-10: 0-7368-3846-5; ISBN-13: 9780736838467

The Brave Escape of Ellen and William Craft (2006)
By Donnie Lemke
ISBN-10: 0-7368-4973-4; ISBN-13: 9780736849739

Buffalo Soldiers and the American West (2006)
By Jason Glaser
ISBN-10: 0-7368-4966-1; ISBN-13: 9780736849661

The Building of the Transcontinental Railroad (2007)
By Nathan Olson
ISBN-10: 0-7368-6490-3; ISBN-13: 9780736864909

The Creation of the U.S. Constitution (2007)
By Michael Burgan
ISBN-10: 0-7368-6491-1; ISBN-13: 9780736864916

The Curse of King Tut's Tomb (2005)
By Michael Burgan
ISBN-10: 0-7368-3833-3; ISBN-13: 9780736838337

Dolley Madison Saves History (2006)
By Roger Smalley
ISBN 13: 9780736849722/ 0-7368-4972-6

Harriet Tubman and the Underground Railroad (2005)
By Michael Martin
ISBN-10: 9780736838290; ISBN-10: 0-7368-3829-5

John Brown's Raid on Harpers Ferry (2006)
By Jason Glaser
ISBN-10: 0-7368-4369-8; ISBN 13: 9780736843690

John Sutter and the California Gold Rush (2006)
By Matt Doeden
ISBN-10: 0-7368-4370-1; ISBN 13: 9780736843706

The Lewis and Clark Expedition (2007)
By Jessica Gunderson
ISBN-10: 0-7368-6493-8; ISBN 13: 9780736864930

Lords of the Sea: The Vikings Explore the North Atlantic (2006)
By Allison Lassieur
ISBN-10: 0-7368-4974-2; ISBN 13: 9780736849746

The Mystery of the Roanoke Colony (2007)
By Xavier Niz
ISBN-10: 0-7368-6494-6; ISBN 13: 9780736864947

Nat Turner's Slave Rebellion (2006)
By Michael Burgan
ISBN-10: 0-7368-5490-8; ISBN 13: 9780736854900

Paul Revere's Ride (2005)
By Xavier Niz
ISBN-10: 0-7368-4965-3; ISBN 13: 9780736849654

The Pilgrims and the First Thanksgiving (2007)
By Mary Englar
ISBN-10: 0-7368-5492-4; ISBN 13: 9780736854924

Rosa Parks and the Montgomery Bus Boycott (2007)
By Connie Colwell Miller
ISBN-10: 0-7368-6495-4; ISBN 13: 9780736864954

The Salem Witch Trials (2005)
By Michael Martin
ISBN-10: 0-7368-3847-3; ISBN 13: 9780736838474

The Sinking of the Titanic (2005)
By Matt Doeden
ISBN-10: 0-7368-3834-1; ISBN 13: 9780736838344

The Story of Jamestown (2006)
By Eric Braun
ISBN-10: 0-7368-4967-X; ISBN 13: 9780736849678

The Story of the Star-Spangled Banner (2006)
By Ryan Jacobson
ISBN-10: 0-7368-5493-2; ISBN 13: 9780736854931

The Story of the Statue of Liberty (2006)
By Xavier Niz
ISBN-10: 0-7368-5494-0; ISBN 13: 9780736854948

The Voyage of the Mayflower Liberty (2006)
By Allison Lassieur
ISBN-10: 0-7368-4371-X; ISBN 13: 9780736843713

Winter at Valley Forge (2005)
By Matt Doeden
ISBN-10: 0-7368-4975-0; ISBN 13: 9780736849753

Young Riders of the Pony Express (2006)
By Jessica Sarah Gunderson
ISBN-10: 0-7368-5495-9; ISBN 13: 9780736854955

Many of Capstone's Graphic History titles are also available in Spanish. These include:

Amos de los mares: los vikingos exploran el Atlantico Norte (The Vikings Explore the North Atlantic) (2007)
By Allison Lassieur
ISBN-10: 0-7368-4974-2; ISBN 13: 9780736849746

Betsy Ross y la bandera de los Estados Unidos (Betsy Ross and the American Flag) (2007)
By Kay Melchisedech Olson
ISBN-10: 0-7368-6614-0; ISBN-13: 9780736866149

Dolley Madison salva la historia (Dolley Madison Saves History) (2007)
By Roger Smalley
ISBN-10: 0-7368-6618-3; ISBN-13: 9780736866187

El asesinato de Abraham Lincoln (The Assassination of Abraham Lincoln) (2006)
By Kay Melchisedech Olson
ISBN-10: 0-7368-6055-X ; ISBN-13: 9780736860550

El hundimiento del Titanic (The Sinking of the Titanic) (2006)
By Matt Doeden
ISBN-10: 0-7368-6061-4; ISBN-13: 9780736860611

El invierno en Valley Forge (Winter at Valley Forge) (2007)
By Matt Doeden
ISBN-10: 0-7368-6621-3; ISBN-13: 9780736866217

El Motin del Te de Boston (The Boston Tea Party) (2006)
By Matt Doeden
ISBN-10: 0-7368-6057-6; ISBN-13: 9780736860574

El valiente escape de Ellen y William Craft (The Brave Escape of Ellen and William Craft)) (2007)
By Donald B. Lemke
ISBN-10: 0-7368-6619-1; ISBN-13: 9780736866194

El viaje del Mayflower (The Voyage of the Mayflower) (2007)
By Matt Doeden
ISBN-10: 0-7368-6613-2; ISBN-13: 9780736866132

Harriet Tubman y el ferrocarril clandestino (Harriet Tubman and the Underground Railroad) (2006)
By Michael Martin
ISBN-10: 0-7368-6059-2; ISBN-13: 9780736860598

John Brown: el ataque a Harpers Ferry (John Brown's Raid on Harpers Ferry) (2007)
By Jason Glaser
ISBN-10: 0-7368-6611-6; ISBN-13: 9780736866118

John Sutter y la fiebre del oro en California (John Sutter and the California Gold rush) (2007)
By Matt Doeden
ISBN 13: 9780736866125; ISBN-10: 0-7368-6612-4

La batalla del Alamo (The Battle of the Alamo) (2006)
By Matt Doeden
ISBN-13: 9780736860567; ISBN-10: 0-7368-6056-8

La Cabalgata de Paul Revere (Paul Revere's Ride) (2007)
By Xavier Niz
ISBN-10: 0-7368-6616-7; ISBN-13: 9780736866163

La historia de Jamestown (The Story of Jamestown) (2007)
By Eric Braun
ISBN-10: 0-7368-6617-5; ISBN-13: 9780736866170

La maldicion de la tumba del Faraon Tut (The Curse of King Tut's Tomb) (2006)
By Michael Burgan
ISBN-10: 0-7368-6058-4; ISBN-13: 9780736860581

La masacre de Boston (The Boston Massacre) (2007)
By Michael Burgan
ISBN-10: 0-7368-6610-8; ISBN-13: 9780736866101

Las aventuras de Marco Polo (The Adventures of Marco Polo) (2006)
Smalley, Roger
ISBN-10: 0-7368-6054-1; ISBN-13: 9780736860543

Los juicios por brujeria en Salem (The Salem Witch Trials) (2006)
By Michael Martin
ISBN-13: 9780736860604; ISBN-10: 0-7368-6060-6

Los soldados de Bufalo y el Oeste Americano (The Buffalo Soldiers and the American West) (2007)
By Jason Glaser
ISBN-10: 0-7368-6615-9; ISBN-13: 9780736866156

Capstone Graphic Library: Graphic Science Series

The Shocking World of Electricity with Max Axiom, Super Scientist (2007)

By Liam O'Donnell
ISBN-10: 0-7368-6835-6; ISBN-13: 9780736868358

As he is walking through his home, Super Scientist Max Axiom shocks himself on a metal doorknob after walking across the carpet. Using this as an example, he goes on to explain how electricity is everywhere in our world. He shrinks down to show young readers the breakdown of an atom (including protons, neutrons, and electrons) and how each electron carries electrical energy called a charge. He explains how friction (e.g., when his socks rub against the carpet) can cause electrons to jump from one atom to another and how these charged electrons can travel through his body, thereby attracting positive atoms in the doorknob—all of which caused that static shock he felt when he grabbed the doorknob. He then takes the reader on a tour of a power plant, explaining how we convert energy to electricity. He also talks about power lines, conductors, circuitry, and resistors. He ends the tour with a brief speech about conserving energy and being a good steward of our natural resources. A lot of information is packed in these 32 pages, and young readers who have an interest in science will be thrilled with these high-interest titles that take a complex subject like electricity and make it very easy to understand. Grades 4 and up.

The Shocking World of Electricity with Max Axiom, Super Scientist by Liam O'Donnell, Richard Dominguez, and Charles Barnett III. Reprinted with permission.

Capstone's "Graphic Library: Graphic Science" Series also include the following books:

Adventures in Sound with Max Axiom, Super Scientist (2007)
By Emily Sohn
ISBN-10: 0-7368-6836-4; ISBN-13: 9780736868365

Attractive Story of Magnetism with Max Axiom, Super Scientist (2008)
By Andrea Gianopoulos
ISBN-10: 1-4296-0141-8; ISBN-13: 9781429601412

A Crash Course in Forces and Motion with Max Axiom, Super Scientist (2007)
By Emily Sohn
ISBN-10: 0-7368-6837-2; ISBN-13: 9780736868372

Exploring Ecosystems with Max Axiom, Super Scientist (2007)
By Agnieszka Biskup
ISBN-10: 0-7368-6842-9; ISBN-13: 9780736868426

Explosive World of Volcanoes with Max Axiom, Super Scientist (2008)
By Christopher L. Harbo
ISBN-10: 1-4296-0144-2; ISBN-13: 9781429601443

Illuminating World of Light with Max Axiom, Super Scientist (2008)
By Emily Sohn
ISBN-10: 1-4296-0140-X; ISBN-13: 9781429601405

A Journey into Adaptation with Max Axiom, Super Scientist (2007)
By Agniesezka Biskup
ISBN-10: 0-7368-6840-2; ISBN-13: 978073686840

Lessons in Science Safety with Max Axiom, Super Scientist (2007)
By Donald B. Lemke and Thomas K. Adamson
ISBN-10: 0-7368-6834-8; ISBN-13: 9780736868341

Understanding Global Warming with Max Axiom, Super Scientist (2008)
By Agniesezka Biskup
ISBN-10: 1-4296-0139-6; ISBN-13: 9781429601399

Understanding Photosynthesis with Max Axiom, Super Scientist (2007)
By Liam O'Donnell
ISBN-10: 0736868410; ISBN-13: 978-0736868419

The World of Food Chains with Max Axiom, Super Scientist (2007)
By Liam O'Donnell
ISBN-10: 0-7368-6839-9; ISBN-13: 9780736868396

Each title in Capstone's "Graphic Library: Graphic Science" series features the fictional Max Axiom, a Super Scientist who was hit by a megacharged lightning bolt when he was younger. When Max woke up after the accident, he discovered he had super powers including extreme intelligence and the ability to shrink down to the size of an atom. He also has some super cool gadgets like his sunglasses which give him x-ray vision and his lab coat, which allows him to travel through space and time. In each book in this series Max travels across globe to study the many disciplines of science including physics, earth science, biology, engineering, geology, and more. Each volume in this ongoing series includes general, factual information about a subject told in a fictional narrative.

Capstone Graphic Library: Disasters in History Series

The Donner Party (2006)
By Scott Welveart, Ron Frenz, and Charles Barnett III
Publisher: Capstone Press
SBN-10: 0-7368-5479-7; ISBN-13: 9780736854795

Like most of the stories in this series about true-life catastrophes, the tragic tale of the Donner Party will hook the most reluctant reader from the start. Victims of a tragic attempt to reach California from Missouri in 1846, 41 of the 87 people on this expedition died before the group was rescued from the Sierra Nevada Mountains in 1847. All of the books in this series present factual information in a developmentally appropriate manner, without being overly sentimental or

Capstone's "Graphic Library: Disasters in History" series also include the following books:

1918 Flu Pandemic (2008)
By Katherine Krohn
Publisher: Capstone Press
ISBN-10: 1-4296-0158-2; ISBN-13: 9781429601580

The Apollo 13 Mission
By Donald B. Lemke
Publisher: Capstone Press
ISBN-10: 0-7368-5476-2; ISBN-13: 9780736854764

The Attack on Pearl Harbor (2006)
By Jane Sutcliffe
Publisher: Capstone Press
ISBN-10: 0-7368-5477-0; ISBN-13: 9780736854771

The Challenger Explosion
By Heather Adamson
Publisher: Capstone Press
ISBN-10: 0-7368-5478-9; ISBN-13: 9780736854788

The Great Chicago Fire of 1871 (2006)
By Kay Melchisedech Olson
Publisher: Capstone Press
ISBN-10: 0-7368-5480-0; ISBN-13: 9780736854801

The Great San Francisco Earthquake and Fire (2008)
By Michael Burgan
Publisher: Capstone Press
ISBN-10: 1-4296-0155-8; ISBN-13: 9781429601559

The Hindenburg Disaster
By Matt Doeden
Publisher: Capstone Press
ISBN-10: 0-7368-5481-9; ISBN-13: 9780736854818

Schoolchildren's Blizzard (2008)
By Donald B. Lemke
Publisher: Capstone Press
ISBN-10: 1-4296-0157-4; ISBN-13: 9781429601573

Shackleton and the Lost Antarctic Expedition (2006)
By B.A. Hoeana
Publisher: Capstone Press
ISBN-10: 0-7368-5482-7; ISBN-13: 9780736854825

The Triangle Shirtwaist Factory Fire (2006)
By Jessica Sarah Gunderson
Publisher: Capstone Press
ISBN-13: 9780736854825; ISBN-13: 9780736854832

skipping relevant parts of the story, even those that may be controversial. For example, it is a documented fact that members of the Donner Party had to resort to cannibalism in order to survive. This is not pleasant, but it's important that it is acknowledged in a nonfiction series about natural disasters. It is just as important that, in a series for children, this information is presented very carefully and without too much graphic detail. It's this kind of honesty and factual presentation of information that will make this series such a draw for young readers, especially boys who are often more drawn to action-oriented nonfiction. Grades 4 and up.

Capstone Graphic Library: Inventions and Discoveries Series

Steve Jobs, Steven Wozniak and the Personal Computer (2007)
By Donald B. Lemke Tod Smith, and Al Milgrom
ISBN-10: 0-7368-6488-1; ISBN-13: 9780736864886

Many young readers may not be familiar with Steve Jobs or Steve Wozniak, but I guarantee that they all know about their invention because most of them have a personal computer in their home or classroom. Technology has changed our world so fast that it's easy to forget that computers have not always been household items, especially if you're under the age of 12 and have never lived in a world without computers and the

Internet. This graphic novel provides young readers with a timeline for the development of the personal computer, beginning with how the two Steves met and how they spent many years creating and testing various prototypes of electronic devices that utilized microprocessors. In 1976, Steve and Steve formed the Apple Computer Company. A year later they had created a logo, developed a comprehensive marketing plan, and debuted the

Apple II Personal Computer to the world. Within months they had sold thousands of computers, but this didn't stop them from refining the product and making changes that would make the personal computer more user friendly, including the development of a disk drive and a graphical user interface. In 1984, they introduced the Apple Macintosh, the first affordable personal computer available to the general public. Grades 4 and up.

 Capstone's "Graphic Library: Inventions and Discoveries" series also include the following books:

Alexander Graham Bell and the Telephone (2007)
By Jennifer Fandel
ISBN-10: 0-7368-6478-4; ISBN-13: 9780736864787

Charles Darwin and the Theory of Evolution (2008)
By Heather Adamson
ISBN-10: 1-4296-0145-0; ISBN-13: 9781429601450

Eli Whitney and the Cotton Gin (2007)
By Jessica Gunderson
ISBN-10: 0-7368-6843-7; ISBN-13: 9780736868433

Frank Zamboni and the Ice-Resurfacing Machine (2008)
By Kay M. Olson
ISBN-10: 1-4296-0147-7; ISBN-13: 9781429601474

George Eastman and the Kodak Camera (2007)
By Jennifer Fandel
ISBN-10: 0-7368-6848-8; ISBN-13: 9780736868488

Hedy Lamarr and a Secret Communication System (2007)
By Trina Robbins
ISBN-10: 0-7368-6479-2; ISBN-13: 9780736864794

Henry Ford and the Model T (2007)
By Michael O'Hearn
ISBN-10: 0-7368-6480-6; ISBN-13: 9780736864800

Isaac Newton and the Laws of Motion (2007)
By Andrea Gianopoulos
ISBN-10: 0-7368-6847-X; ISBN-13: 9780736868471

Jake Burton Carpenter and the Snowboard (2007)
By Michael O'Hearn
ISBN-10: 0-7368-6481-4; ISBN-13: 9780736864817

Johann Gutenberg and the Printing Press (2007)

By Kay Melchisedech Olson
ISBN-10: 0-7368-6482-2; ISBN-13: 9780736864824

Jonas Salk and the Polio Vaccine (2007)
By Al Milgrom
ISBN-10: 0-7368-6483-0; ISBN-13: 9780736864831

Levi Strauss and Blue Jeans (2007)
By Nathan Olson
ISBN-10: 0-7368-6484-9; ISBN-13: 9780736864848

Louis Pasteur and Pasteurization (2007)
By Jennifer Fandel
ISBN-10: 0-7368-6844-5; ISBN-13: 9780736868440

Madam C .J. Walker and New Cosmetics (2007)
By Katherine Krohn
ISBN-10: 0-7368-6485-7; ISBN-13: 9780736864855

Marie Curie and Radioactivity (2007)
By Connie Colwell Miller
ISBN-10: 0-7368-6486-5; ISBN-13: 9780736864862

Philo Farnsworth and the Television (2007)
By Ellen Sturm Niz
ISBN-10: 0-7368-6487-3; ISBN-13: 9780736864879

Samuel Morse and the Telegraph (2007)
By David Seidman
ISBN-10: 0-7368-6846-1; ISBN-13: 9780736868464

Thomas Edison and the Lightbulb (2007)
By Scott R. Welvaert
ISBN-10: 0-7368-6489-X; ISBN-13: 9780736864893

The Wright Brothers and the Airplane (2007)
By Xavier Niz
ISBN-10: 0-7368-6845-3; ISBN-13: 9780736868457

Z-Boys and Skateboarding (2008)
By Jameson Anderson
ISBN-10: 1-4296-0150-7; ISBN-13: 9781429601504

Appendix A: Glossary

Anime (awn-ee-may) The Japanese term for animation. The word anime is derived from the French word animé, which means animated or lively.

Cartoon This term is most often used to refer to animated television shows in North America. It can also be used to refer to a (usually humorous) drawing in a newspaper or magazine that is intended to symbolize, satirize, or characterize a person, place, or event (e.g., a political cartoon).

Comic In this book, the term "comic" is used as a catch all phrase for all books created in a comic format.

Comic Book A traditional, staple bound, serialized pamphlet or periodical that tells a story using sequential art.

Comic Strip Varying from one to several panels, this is the comic format that appears in newspapers and magazines. Most comic strips do not have continuing story lines.

Graphic Novel Term coined by artist/writer Will Eisner in 1978. A graphic novel is a book-length story that is written and illustrated in a comic-book style. It can be an original, self-contained story or it can be a collection of previously published comic books that together tell one story. It can also be an original publication that features traditional comic book characters.

Manga (mawn-guh) Japanese comics in print form that traditionaly read back to front, right to left.

Manga Style A term used to describe graphic novels created outside of Japan that utilize a manga style and format, including traditional manga trim size, black and white art, and stylistic elements common to manga that include simple drawings, characters with large eyes, over-exaggerated emotions, the use of fewer words to tell the story, and the use of symbols to convey emotions.

Manhwa (man-wah) Korean comics in print form that are similar to manga, but read front to back, left to right.

Neo-Manga Another name for graphic novels originally written in English that are created in a manga-style front to back, left to right format. Neo-manga reads front to back, left to right, like traditional books written in the English language. See also OEL manga.

OEL Manga Original English Language manga. This term was coined by Tokyopop to differentiate American/English graphic novels created in a manga style format from traditional, Japanese manga. OEL manga reads front to back, left to right, like traditional books written in the English language. See also Neo-manga.

Shojo (show-joe) A Japanese term used to describe manga or anime primarily aimed at a young female audience under the age of 18. These books are typically written by women and usually tend to be more character based. They also traditionally focus on romance from a young female perspective and emotions and social interaction are a prominent part of the story. Also spelled Shoujo.

Shonen (show-nen) A Japanese term used to describe manga or anime for boys under the age of 18, although many older men enjoy these stories. These series usually focus on action, sports, or romance from a male perspective and usually feature strong action-themed stories with male protagonists.

Trim Size The final size of a printed page, often used to describe the size of a book (e.g., traditional trim size for manga is 5 in x 7.5 in).

Visual Literacy The ability to recognize and understand ideas conveyed through visual (still or animated) imagery.

Appendix B: Online Resource Guides

Comics in the Classroom
<http://www.comicsintheclassroom.net>

Created by a teacher from New Brunswick, Canada, this site includes lesson plans, recommend titles for elementary- aged readers, a list of kid-friendly comic book retailers, a forum for online communication, and news from the comic publishing industry about comics for kids.

Diamond Bookshelf
<http://bookshelf.diamondcomics.com/public/>

This site has a little bit of everything for both school and public librarians including information about starting a new collection, cataloging, lesson plans, reaching reluctant readers, reviews of hot new titles, and more. You can even download a free copy of the "Graphic Novels and Libraries" resource guide here, which includes recommended titles, collection development tips, and lesson plans.

The Graphic Classroom
<http://graphicclassroom.blogspot.com/>

This site is actually a blog, or online journal, created and maintained by Chris Wilson, who is working on his Masters of Science Degree in Education at the College of Education at Missouri State University. The blog highlights graphic novels and comics that can be added to the classroom and/or school library, specifically all age comics that can be used in the Elementary classroom. Chris does very detailed reviews of each graphic novel, as well as content area recommendations for using these books in the classroom.

Kid-Safe Graphic Novels for Younger Readers
<http://www.graphicnovels.brodart.com/>

This site (sponsored by Brodart) includes core lists, guidelines for selecting kid-safe graphic novels, selection criteria, new and notable titles, links to article about graphic novels in libraries, and more.

Scholastic Graphix Site
<http://www.scholastic.com/graphix/>

Graphix is Scholastic's graphic novels imprint for young readers. This site includes a link to a teaching guide for using comics in the classroom, a message board, a blog, and activities for kids, including a site to create your own comic book by choosing a layout, selecting images, and adding text.

Sidekicks!
<http://sidekicks.noflyingnotights.com/>

A sister site to the very well-known No Flying! No Tights! Web site, Sidekicks! contains reviews of graphic novels for younger readers. Created and maintained by No Flying! No Tights! creator Robin Brenner, this site is a great resource for reviews of recommended titles for young children and preteen readers.

Secret Origin of Good Readers Resource Book
<http://www.night-flight.com/secretorigin/>

This 60+ page resource (free to download as a pdf file) includes lesson plans, core lists, and more. It's worth the download time. Scroll down to the bottom of the page to find the link to the latest download.

Kids Love Comics!
<http://kidslovecomics.com/>

Founded by Jimmy Gownley (creator of Amelia Rules!) and Harold Buchholz (creator of Apathy Kat), Kids Love Comics is a non-profit organization made up of comic creators, publishers, fans, educators and journalists, as well as those involved in the marketing, promotion, distribution, and retail of the comic book medium. The goal of this site is to provide readers with the latest news, links, and events related to kid-friendly comics!

Appendix C: Professional Books about Graphic Novels

Although not all of these books address comics specifically for younger readers, they do offer a wealth of information about developing a collection of graphic novels, recommended titles for reader's advisory, programming ideas, and information about using graphic novels in the classroom and with reluctant readers and English as a Second Language readers.

101 Best Graphic Novels
By Stephen Weiner
Publisher: NBM Publishing
ISBN: 156163283X

Building Literacy Connections with Graphic Novels: Page by Page, Panel by Panel
By James Bucky Carter
Publisher: National Council of Teachers of English
ISBN: 0814103928

Developing and Promoting Graphic Novel Collections (Teens @ the Library Series)
By Steve Miller
Publisher: Neal-Schuman
ISBN: 15557046161

Getting Graphic! Using Graphic Novels to Promote Literacy with Preteens and Teens
By Michele Gorman
Publisher: Linworth Publishing
ISBN: 1586830899

Going Graphic: Comics at Work in the Multilingual Classroom
By Stephen Cary
Publisher: Heinemann
ISBN: 0-325-00475-7

Graphic Novels: A Genre Guide to Comics, Manga, and More
By Michael Pawuk
Publisher: Libraries Unlimited
ISBN: 1-598158-132-x

Graphic Novels in Your Media Center: A Definitive Guide
By Allyson W. Lyga and Barry Lyga
Publisher: Libraries Unlimited
ISBN: 1591581427

Graphic Novels Now: Building, Managing, and Marketing (a Dynamic Collection)
By Francisca Goldsmith
Publisher: American Library Association
ISBN: 0838909043

Understanding Manga and Anime
By Robin E. Brenner
Publisher: Libraries Unlimited
ISBN: 159158332

Works Cited

Griepp, Milton. "The New Trends in Shaping Pop Culture." ICv2 Graphic Novel Conference. February 22, 2007. New York Comic Con. New York City. ICv2 White Paper–Graphic Novel Growth and Change.

"Manga Surge on the Horizon." 6 July 2007. ICv2. Accessed 6 August 2007 <http://www.icv2.com/articles/news/10866.html>.

Masessa, Ed. "The New Trends in Shaping Pop Culture." ICv2 Graphic Novel Conference. February 22, 2007. New York Comic Con. New York City. Buyers Panel–The Next Three Years.

Combined Index

A

Adamson, Heather 70, 75, 76
Adamson, Thomas K. 74
Adventures in Oz 1, 2
Adventures in Sound with Max Axiom, Super Scientist 82, 73, 74
Adventures of Marco Polo, The 82
Adventures of Polo, The 1
Adventures of TinTin, The 3
Adventures of Tom Sawyer, The 17
Akiko Pocket Size by Mark Crilley 3
Alexander Graham Bell and the Telephone 76
Alfonso, Jose 17
Alia's Mission: Saving the Books of Iraq 57
Alison Dare: Little Miss Adventures 3
Amano, Shiro 49, 50
Amaterasu: Return of the Sun 57, 58, 59
Ambrosio, Stefano 25
Amelia Earhart: Free in the Skies 61, 62
Amelia Earhart: Legendary Aviator 67
Amelia Rules! iv-vii, 4, 5, 78
Amos de los mares: los vikingos exploran el Atlantico Norte 71
Anderson, Jameson 67, 76
Aoki, Takao 42
Apollo 13 Mission, The 75
Artemis Fowl: The Graphic Novel 4, 31
Arthur & Lancelot: The Fight for Camelot 59
Asesinato de Abraham Lincoln, El 71
Assassination of Abraham Lincoln, The 70
Atalanta: The Race Against Destiny 59
Atlantis: The Mystery of the Lost City 66
Attack on Pearl Harbor, The 75
Attractive Story of Magnetism with Max Axiom, Super Scientist 74
Avatar: The Last Airbender 48
Avengers and Power Pack Digest 4
Aventuras de Marco Pol, Las 72
Azuma, Kiyohiko 46, 47

B

B.B. Explosion 39
BABYMOUSE 6, 7, 11
Baby Sitter's Club, The 6
Barbieri, Carlo 15
Barks, Carl 10, 18
Barnett, Charles 67, 73, 74
Baron the Cat Returns 39
Barry, James 53
Batalla del Alamo, La 72
Batman Strikes, The 6, 15
Battle of Gettysburg, The 70
Battle of the Alamo, The 70
Beatty, Terry 6
Beck, Jerry 14
Beechen, Adam 15, 32
Beet the Vandel Buster 41

Benedict Arnold 67
Benjamin Franklin: An American Genius 67
Benjamin Franklin: un genio norteamericano 69
Beowulf: Monster Slayer 59
Bermuda Triangle: The Disappearance of Flight 19, The 66
Bessie Coleman 67
Best of Pokemon Adventures, The 41
Betsy Ross and the American Flag 70
Betsy Ross y la bandera de los Estados Unidos 71
Battle of the Bulge: Turning Back Hitler's Final Push, The 61
BeyBlade 42
Big Fat Little Lit 18, 20
Bigfoot: A North American Legend 66
Biker Girl 48
Biskup, Agnieszeka 74
Bit Haywire, A 8
Black Beauty 17
Blevins, Bertt 27
Bone iii, ix, 8, 9, 30
Bone, J. 3
Booker T. Washington: gran educador norteamericano 69
Booker T. Washington: Great American Educator 67
Boston Massacre, The 70, 72
Boston Tea Party, The 70
Boy, the Bear, the Baron, the Bard, The 10
Braun, Eric 67, 68, 69, 71, 72
Brave Escape of Ellen and William Craft, The 70
Brenner, Robin ii, 38, 78, 79
Buchholz, Harold 78
Buffalo Soldiers and the American West 70
Building of the Transcontinental Railroad, The 70
Bullock, Mike 18, 19
Burgan, Michael 17, 67, 68, 70, 71, 72, 75
Burleigh, Robert 61, 62
Buzzboy: Sidekicks Rule! 10

C

Cabalgata de Paul Revere, La 72
Cabarga, Leslie 14
Calero, Dennis 17
Captain Raptor and the Moon Mystery 10
Card Captor Sakura 42
Carl Barks' Greatest Duck Tales Stories 10
Carroll, Lewis 52
Carruthers, Sandy 59
Carter, James Bucky 79
Cary, Stephen x, 11, 79
Cesar Chavez: Fighting for Farmworkers 68
Cesar Chavez: lucha por los trabajadores del campo 69
Chabot, Jacob 21
Challenger Explosion, The 75
Charles Darwin and the Theory of Evolution 76
Christopher Columbus 68
Cibos, Lindsay 53
CLAMP 42

Clan Apis 62, 63
Clara Barton: Angel del campo de batalla 69
Clara Barton: Angel of the Battlefield 68
Clugston, Chynna 27
Cockcroft, Jason 59
Coleman, Wim 17
Colfer, Eoin 4
Comic Zone: Kid Gravity 11
Courageous Princess 11, 12
*Crash Course in Forces and Motion with Max
 Axiom, Super Scientist, A* 79
Creation of the U.S. Constitution, The 70
Crilley, Mark 3
Croall, Marie P. 59
Curse of King Tut's Tomb, The 70
Czekaj, Jef 13

D

David, Erica
Davis, Terry 17
De Campi, Alex 49
Debon, Nicholas 64
DeFalco, Tom
Demeter & Persephone: Spring Held Hostage 59
DeMolay, Jack 66
Denton, Shannon 55
Dezago, Todd 32
Di Gi Charat 43
Di Martino, Michael Dante 48
Difiori, Lawrence 14
Doeden, Matt 68, 69, 70, 71, 72
Dolley Madison salva la historia 71
Dolley Madison Saves History 70
Donbo, Koge 43
Donkin, Andrew 4
Donner Party, The 74
Drawing Comics is Easy (Except When It's Hard) 62

E

Elder, Joshua 50, 51
Eleanor Roosevelt: First Lady of the World 68
Eleanor Roosevelt: primera dama del mundo 69
Eli Whitney and the Cotton Gin 76
Elizabeth Blackwell: America's First Woman Doctor 68
*Elizabeth Cady Stanton: pionera de los derechos de
 las mujeres* 69
Elizabeth Cady Stanton: Women's Rights Pioneer 68
Engfer, Lee 68
Englar, Mary 71
Erwin, Steve 67
ESL x, xi
Espinoza, Rod 11, 12, 52
*Exploring Ecosystems with Max Axiom, Super
 Scientist* 74
*Explosive World of Volcanoes with Max Axiom,
 Super Scientist* 74

F

Faller, Regis 1, 2
Fandel, Jennifer 68, 76
Fashion Kitty 11
First Moon Landing, The 70
Florence Nightingale 68
Flu Pandemic, 1918 75
Fontes, Justine 59
Fontes, Ron 59
Frampton, Otis 22, 23
Frank Zamboni and the Ice-Resurfacing Machine 76
Frankenstein 17
Frenz, Ron 74

G

Gallagher, John 10
Gallagher, Mike 53
George Eastman and the Kodak Camera 76
George Washington Carver: Ingenious Inventor 68
George Washington: dirigiendo una nueva nacion 69
George Washington: Leading a New Nation 68
Ghosts of Amityville: The Haunted House, The 66
Gianopoulos, Andrea 74, 76
Giffen, Keith 55
Glaser, Jason 68, 69, 70, 72
Goldsmith, Francisca 79
Gon 43
Goosebumps Graphix 11
Gownley, Jimmy ii, iv, 4, 5, 78
Grampa & Julie: Shark Hunters 13
Great Chicago Fire of 1871, The 75
Great San Francisco Earthquake and Fire, The 75
Griepp, Milton 37, 80
Guibert, Emmanuel 29
Gunderson, Jessica 68, 70, 71, 75, 76
Gurihiru 4, 27, 30, 35

H

H.G. Wells's Time Machine 17
Hall, M.C. 15, 16, 17
Harbo, Christopher L. 74
Hardy Boys Series, The 13
Harper, Charise Mericle 11
Harriet Tubman and the Underground Railroad 70
Harriet Tubman y el ferrocarril clandestino 72
Harvey Comics Classics, Volume 1: Casper 14
Hedy Lamarr and a Secret Communication System 76
Helen Keller: Courageous Advocate 68
Helen Keller: valiente defensora 69
Henry Ford and the Model T 76
Hercules: The Twelve Labors 59
Herge 3
Hernandez, Gabriel
Herobear and the Kid: The Inheritance 14
Hiiragi, Aoi 39
Hikaru No Go 43, 44
Hima, Larry 61
Hindenburg Disaster, The 75
Historia de Jamestown, La 72
Hodges, Jared 53
Hoena, B.A. 68, 69
Holm, Jennifer L. 6, 7

Holm, Matthew 6. 7
Horowitz, Anthony 31
Horumarin 45
Hosler, Jay 62, 63
Hotta, Yumi 43, 44
Huddleston, Courtney 8
Hugo, Victor 17
Hulk and Power Pack: Pack Smash 14
Hunchback of Notre Dame, The 17
Hundimiento del Titanic, El 71
Hunter, Erin 53, 54
Hutchison, David 52

I

Ikumi, Mia 46
Illuminating World of Light with Max Axiom,
Super Scientist 74
Imai, Yasue 39
Inada, Koji 41
Inada, Riku 41
Into the Air: The Story of the Wright Brothers' First
Flight 62
Invierno en Valley Forge, El 71
Invisible Man, The 17
Isis & Osiris: To the Ends of the Earth 59
Isaac Newton and the Laws of Motion 76

J

Jackie and the Shadow Snatcher 14
Jackie Robinson: Baseball's Great Pioneer 68
Jackie Robinson: gran pionero del beisbol 69
Jacobson, Ryan 68, 69, 71
Jacques, Brian 21, 27
Jake Burton Carpenter and the Snowboard 76
Jane Goodall: Animal Scientist 68
Jason: Quest for the Golden Fleece 59
Jetcat Clubhouse 15
Jim Thorpe: Greatest Athlete in the World 68
Johann Gutenberg and the Printing Press 76
John Brown: el ataque a Harpers Ferry 72
John Brown's Raid on Harpers Ferry 70
John F. Kennedy 68
John Sutter and the California Gold Rush 70
John Sutter y la fiebre del oro en California 72
Johnston, Antony 31
Jolley, Dan 34, 53, 54, 59
Jonas Salk and the Polio Vaccine 76
Jones, Christopher 6
Jones, Eric 11
Journey into Adaptation with Max Axiom, Super
Scientist, A 74
Journey to the Center of the Earth 17
Juicios por brujeria en Salem, Los 72
Justice League Unlimited 15

K

Kat & Mouse 49
Khron, Katherine E. 68
King Arthur and the Knights of the Round Table
15, 16
King Arthur: Excalibur Unsheathed 59
Kingdom Hearts 37, 49

Kingdom Hearts: Chain of Memories 50
Kitchen, Alexa S. 62
Konietzko, Bryan 48
Korgi, Volume 1: Sprouting Wings 15
Krohn, Katherine 75, 76
Kruse, Jason T. 35, 36
Kunkel, Mike 14
Kurth, Steve 59
Kusaka, Hidenori 41

L

Lassieur, Allison 68, 69, 70, 71
Lawrence, Jack 18, 19
Leave it to Chance 17
Lechner, John 31
Legend of Hong Kil Dong: The Robin Hood of
Korea, The 18
Lemke, Donnie B. 70, 71, 74, 75
Lentz, Bob 68
Lervold, Eric 32
Lessons in Science Safety with Max Axiom,
Super Scientist 74
Levi Strauss and Blue Jeans 76
Lewis and Clark Expedition, The 70
Life and Times of Scrooge McDuck, The 18
Limke, Jeff 59
Lions, Tigers and Bears, Volume 1: Fear And Pride
18, 19
Little Lit 18, 20
Little Lulu Color Special 20
Lobdell, Scott 13
Loch Ness Monster: Scotland's Mystery Beast, The 66
Lords of the Sea: The Vikings Explore the North
Atlantic 70
Louis Pasteur and Pasteurization 76
Love, Jeremy 29
Love, Robert 29
Lyga, Allyson 79
Lyga, Barry 79

M

Madam C .J. Walker and New Cosmetics 76
Magic Pickle
Mail Order Ninja 50, 51
Maldicion de la tumba del Faraon Tut, La 72
Manak, Dave 53
Manfredi, Ferderica 49
Marie Curie and Radioactivity 76
Martin Luther King, Jr.: Great Civil Rights Leader 68
Martin, Ann M. 6
Marts, Michael 66
Marvel Adventures Fantastic Four 20
Marvel Adventures Spider-Man 20
Masacre de Boston, La 72
Matheny, Bill 6
Mato 41
Matthew Henson: Arctic Adventurer 68
Matthew Henson: aventurero del Artico 69
McCrea, John 59
McKeever, Sean
Medabots 45
Megaman NT Warrior 45
Mighty Skullboy Army, The 21

Milgrom, Al 75, 76
Miller, Connie Colwell 67, 68, 69, 71, 76
Miller, David Worth 17
Miller, Steve 79
Molly Pitcher: Young American Patriot 68
Moore, Stuart 27
Morse, Scott
Mother Jones: Labor Leader 67
Motin del Te de Boston, El 71
Mouly, Françoise 18
Mouse Guard: Fall 1152 21
Muhammad Ali: American Champion 68
Murase, Sho 23
Murray, Doug 61, 62
Mystery of the Roanoke Colony, The 70

N

Naifeh, Ted 25, 26
Nancy Drew Series 23
Nat Turner's Slave Rebellion 71
Nathan Hale: espia revolucionario 69
Nathan Hale: Revolutionary Spy 68
Neotopia Color Manga 52
New Alice in Wonderland Color Manga 52
Niz, Ellen Sturm 76
Niz, Xavier 70, 71, 72, 76

O

O'Brien, Anne Sibley 18
O'Malley, Kevin 10
Oddly Normal 22, 23
O'Donnell, Liam 72, 73, 74
Odysseus: Escaping Poseidon's Curse 59
O'Hearn, Michael 76
Olson, Kay Melchisedech 67, 69, 70, 71, 75, 76
Olson, Nathan 68, 69, 70, 76
Owen, Erich 50, 51
Owens, L. L. 17
Owly 24, 25
Oz: The Manga, Pocket Manga Volume 1 52

P

Pagulayan, Carlo 20
Parme, Fabrice 33
Patrick Henry: Liberty or Death 68
Patrick Henry: muerte o libertad 69
Paul Revere's Ride 71
Pawuk, Mike ii, 79
Peach Fuzz 53
Perrin, Pat 17
Petersen, David 21
Petrucha, Stefan 23
Philo Farnsworth and the Television 76
Pilgrims and the First Thanksgiving, The 71
Pirates of the Caribbean: Dead Man's Chest 25
Polly and the Pirates 25, 26
Power Pack: Pack Attack 27
Purcell, Gordon 59, 70

Q

Q2a 66
Queen Bee 27
Quijada, Sergio 23

R

Randall, Ron 57, 58, 59
Rau, Zachary 32
Rebis, Greg 17
Redwall: The Graphic Novel 27
Rendon, Daniel 13
Renier, Aaron 30
Reynolds, Aaron 32
Richards, C.E. 15, 16
Rigano, Giovanno 4, 25
Riordan, James 59
Robbins, Trina 67, 68, 76
Robin Hood 17
Robin Hood: Outlaw of Sherwood Forest 59
Robinson, James 17
Robot Dreams 27, 28
Rocks, Misako 48
Rogers, Gregory 10
Rosa Parks and the Montgomery Bus Boycott 71
Rosa, Dom 18
Ruiz, Ocampo 17
Runton, Andy 24, 25

S

Sacagawea: Journey into the West 68
Salem Witch Trials, The 71
Samual Adams: Patriot and Statesman 68
Samuel Morse and the Telegraph 76
Sardine in Outer Space 29
Satchel Paige: Striking Out Jim Crow 62
Scary Godmother 29
Scholastic Book Fair ix
Schoolchildren's Blizzard, The 75
Schultz, Barbara 59
Scieszka, Jon 32
Seidman, David 76
Sewell, Anna 17
Sfar, Joann 29
Shackleton and the Lost Antarctic Expedition 75
Shadow Rock 29
Shanower, Eric 1
Shazam! The Monster Society of Evil 30
Shelley, Mary 17, 33
Shepard, Aaron 17
Shocking World of Electricity with Max Axiom,
*   Super Scientist, The* 72, 73
shojo 39, 46, 77
shonen 41, 77
Siegel, Mark ii, 64, 65
Siegel, Sienna Cherson 64, 65
Sinbad: Sailing into Peril 59
Sinking of the Titanic, The 71
Slade, Christian 15
Smalley, Roger 70, 71, 72
Smith, Jeff ii, iii, ix, 8, 9, 30
Smith, Paul 14
Smith, Tod 75
Sohn, Emily 74

Soldados de Bufalo y el Oeste Americano, Los 72
Sonic the Hedgehog Archives 53
Spider-Man and Power Pack: Big City Heroes 30
Spiegelman, Art 18
Spiral Bound 30
Stamaty, Mark Alan 57
Stanley, John 20
Star Wars: Clone Wars Adventures 31
statistics
*Steve Jobs, Steven Wozniak and the Personal
    Computer* 75
Stephens, Jay 15
Stevenson, Robert Louis 17
Sticky Burr: Adventures in Burrwood Forest 31
Stormbreaker: The Graphic Novel 31
Storrie, Paul D. 57, 58, 59
Story of Jamestown, The 71
Story of the Star-Spangled Banner, The 71
Story of the Statue of Liberty, The 71
Strickland, Daniel 17
Strongest Man in the World: Louis Cyr, The 64
Sturm, James 62
Sumerak, Mark 4, 14, 27, 30, 35
Sutcliffe, Jane 75

T

Takamisaki, Ryo 45
Tanaka, Masashi 43
Tanner, Jennifer 17
Teen Titans Go! 32
Telgemeier, Raina 6
Tellos: Gargantua 32
The Trojan Horse: The Fall of Troy 59
*The World of Food Chains with Max Axiom,
    Super Scientist* 74
The Wright Brothers and the Airplane 76
Theodore Roosevelt 68
Theseus: Battling the Minotaur 59
Thomas Edison and the Lightbulb 76
Thomas Jefferson: Great American 68
Thompson, Jill 29
Thor & Loki: The Land of the Giants 59
Tiger Moth 32
Time Warp Trio 32
Tiny Tyrant 33
To Dance: A Ballerina's Graphic Novel 64, 65
Tokyo Mew Mew 46
Tokyo Mew Mew a la Mode 66
Tommaso, Rich 62
Torres, J. 3, 32
Treasure Island 17
Triangle Shirtwaist Factory Fire, The 75
trim size 48, 53, 77
Tripp, Irving 20
Trondheim, Lewis 33
Twain, Mark 17
Twisted Journeys 33, 34

U

UFOs: The Roswell Incident 66
*Understanding Global Warming with Max Axiom,
    Super Scientist* 74
*Understanding Photosynthesis with Max Axiom,
    Super Scientist* 74

V

Valiente escape de Ellen y William Craft, El 71
Varon, Sara 27, 28
Verne, Jules 17
Viaje del Mayflower, El 71
Villavert, Armand 55
visual learner x
visual literacy 77
Voyage of the Mayflower Liberty, The 71

W

W.I.T.C.H. 35
Wade, Mary Dodson 68
Walker, Landry Quinn 11
Warriors 53, 54
Watson, Anne L. 17
Weiner, Stephen 79
Wells, H.G. 17
Welvaert, Scott 68, 69, 74, 76
White, Steve 62
Wieringo, Mike 32
William Penn: Founder of Pennsylvania 68
Williams, Anthony 60, 61
Wilma Rudolph: Olympic Track Star 68
Wilson, Chris 78
Winter at Valley Forge 71
Wong, Walden 15
World of Quest, The 35, 36
Wylie, Bill 62

X

X-Men and Power Pack Digest 35

Y

Yeates, Thomas 59
Yoshida, Akira 20
Yoshida, Reiko 46
Yotsuba&! 46, 47, 48
Young Riders of the Pony Express 71
Yu the Great: Conquering the Flood 59

Z

Zapt! 55
Z-Boys and Skateboarding 76
Zirkel, Scott 8